Cherokee Bill

Black Cowboy—Indian Outlaw

By Art T. Burton

EAKIN PRESS ✦ Fort Worth, Texas
www.EakinPress.com

Copyright © 2020
By Art T. Burton
Published By Eakin Press
An Imprint of Wild Horse Media Group
P.O. Box 331779
Fort Worth, Texas 76163
1-817-344-7036
www.EakinPress.com
ALL RIGHTS RESERVED
1 2 3 4 5 6 7 8 9
ISBN-10: 1-68179-156-0
ISBN-13: 978-1-68179-130-2

Content

The Day They Hung Crawford Goldsby!

By: Wallace C. Moore, Sr. of Lawton, Oklahoma.

Copyright © 2018

This afternoon they hung that young Negro Goldsby boy. I am here to tell you it was a horrible thing to behold.

There must have been over a thousand people that came to see him off. It was a shame, that boy was only twenty-years-old.

Most of the women in the audience were crying. I tell you it was mighty sad.

His mother cried out at the crack of the trap door, "Lord God Almighty. What made my boy go bad?"

At the age of eighteen he shot that Negro boy Jake Lewis. After that he was on a run away horse headed for hell, at break neck speed.

Some say that he was destined to be a killer, they say from the womb to death, he was just a bad seed.

When he killed that Cherokee officer Sequoyah Houston, for a while the law made things mighty hot.

If someone got robbed or somebody got killed, he would be blamed, whether he did it or not.

As he laid in his casket, they all tried to touch him or cut a clip of his hair, They wanted something of his that they could save.

Today when they hung young Crawford Goldsby, they put the Indian outlaw, Cherokee Bill in his grave.

Introduction

Once upon a time in the late nineteenth century, there was an outlaw that captured the imagination of the American public like no other. He can be compared to John Dillinger or Pretty Boy Floyd of the 1930s. Like both of these men, he garnered national press for his exploits; the well known *New York Times* had a running commentary on his actions and deeds. This outlaw's name was Crawford Goldsby, better known as Cherokee Bill. I will refer to him interchangeably in the text, but mostly by the sobriquet Cherokee Bill.

Cherokee Bill was every bit as colorful and outrageous as any criminal of the western frontier, perhaps even more so. There were a few things about him that made him truly unique for a famous desperado of the purple sage. First and foremost, he was an African American living in the Indian Territory. Bill was a descendant of slaves on both sides of his family lineage. The Indian Territory was the home of Indian Freedmen of the Five Civilized Tribes. These were black people, who before the Civil War, had been slaves of the Cherokee, Choctaw, Chickasaw, Creek and Seminole tribes.

Bill was a citizen of the Cherokee Nation, as a freedman, from his mother's lineage. His father was a mulatto from Alabama. We will discuss this more in depth in following chapters. The family name was Goldsby, but it was pronounced, in sound, as Gouldsby or Goosby, and sometimes it was mistakenly spelled as such.

Cherokee Bill was a cowboy; many times outlaws of the

Old West had never worked as true cowboys on the range. But this was common for outlaws of the Indian Territory, pre-statehood Oklahoma, and there were quite a few, black, white and red outlaws who were former cowboys. In researching the history of the Indian Territory, there were a large number of African Americans, many Indian Freedmen, who became outlaws in the Indian Territory. The most famous outlaw of the 1880s, in the Indian Territory was a black man named Dick Glass, who was a Creek Freedman. Cherokee Bill, a Cherokee Freedman, became the most famous outlaw of the 1890s, and arguably the most famous in the history of the Indian Territory. Indians that rivaled Cherokee Bill's notoriety in the Indian Territory would have to include Ned Christie and Henry Starr, both Cherokee.

After the Oklahoma Territory was formed in 1890, the outlaws would cross the borders of the Indian and Oklahoma territories quite frequently going in both directions. They would commit crimes in the "twin territories," running from the deputy U.S. marshals and Indian police in a constant struggle for survival.

The more well known white outlaws were mainly from the Oklahoma Territory, but would commit crimes in the Indian Territory. These would include desperadoes such as the Dalton brothers, Dynamite Dick Clifton, the Christian brothers, and Al Jennings. It should be noted that the Oklahoma Territory was Indian land opened up for settlement in 1889. Large numbers of whites and blacks moved into this land. Although there were black felons in the Oklahoma Territory, none gathered the fame and notoriety as the ones from the Indian Territory, who were principally Indian Freedmen.

I would have to compare Cherokee Bill to Billy the Kid, (Billy Antrim), of New Mexico Territory fame. Although both outlaws received national media attention for their crimes while they were living, Billy the Kid was remembered and immortalized in books and films in the twentieth century, this did not occur for Cherokee Bill. During their criminal careers, both men attempted jail breaks, Billy the Kid was successful, Cherokee Bill was not. Some people have said this is what separated the two from both becoming immortal.

Hollywood has made over forty-five movies on Billy the Kid, and the state of New Mexico has him woven into tourism opportunities all over the state today. When traveling to New Mexico you definitely know you are in "Billy the Kid" country. There were no movies and few books written on Cherokee Bill and if you travel in Oklahoma today, you would never know Cherokee Bill existed.

I would also compare Cherokee Bill to the Depression era outlaw John Dillinger, both became nationally known for their depredations and both of their careers lasted about the same amount of time, a little over a year in length. Dillinger was successful in a jail break, as was Billy the Kid, but Cherokee Bill's attempted jail break, as mentioned earlier was unsuccessful. If Cherokee Bill had been more successful with his attempt, it might have added to his notoriety as it did for Dillinger and the Kid. There were other black outlaws in the Wild West; two rode with Billy the Kid in New Mexico Territory. In the Indian Territory, there was the infamous Dick Glass of the 1880s, but Cherokee Bill became the most famous black outlaw of the Wild West era.

Travel along with me on my narrative journey of Crawford Goldsby *aka* Cherokee Bill; we will examine family history, the political climate in the Indian Territory at the time of his crimes and the national fame that he was able to garner. After much research, I would have to say that Cherokee Bill became the most famous black outlaw of the late nineteenth century, sometimes his nickname made people believe he was a Native American. This was evident later in Hollywood when a western television series highlighted the exploits of Cherokee Bill in one of their programs and identified him as an Indian. This was an episode of *Stories of the Century* which was broadcast in February of 1955. The actor that portrayed Cherokee Bill was an Indian, one of the few Native Americans in Hollywood at that time. His name was Pat Hogan and he was a Pottawatomie/Oneida from Oklahoma. Hogan appeared in many other television programs at that time portraying Indians including Walt Disney's *Davy Crockett King of the Wild Frontier*.

In 1965, the first book on black cowboys was published by authors Philip Durham and Everett L. Jones, titled, *The Negro Cowboy*. They have a description of Cherokee Bill that was gleaned from an earlier book published in 1928, titled, *Warpath and Cattle Trail*, written by Hubert E. Collins. The person Collins wrote about was from the 1870s, took place in the Indian Territory, but was not Crawford Goldsby.

There appears to have been a few cowboys in the late nineteenth century with the moniker of "Cherokee Bill." The one in *Warpath and Cattle Trail* was a black man, but had long flowing hair like Nat Love, *aka* "Deadwood Dick." Crawford Goldsby, the "Cherokee Bill" of the Indian Territory during the 1890s had short kinky hair; common among African Americans. Goldsby's Cherokee Bill would become the most famous of all during the Wild West era. Cherokee Bill was as daring and dangerous as any desperado you will find in the Old West. When it comes to sheer criminality, he took a back seat to no one.

I would like to thank my wife, Patrice, for keeping me on point in regards to finishing this book. If there are any errors in the book, I take all responsibility for them. I would also like to thank Bennie McRae of Columbus, Ohio, for assisting with information on Cherokee Bill. Dessie Preston a relative of George Goldsby was very helpful with information on and photos of her family. Nicka Smith, a descendant of Ike Rogers gave information and photos on the Rogers family. Nikki Yvette Cater, a relative of Maggie Glass, shared photos of her family.

I want to give a big thank you, for all the people who were considerate and shared information for my research. I hope everyone enjoys this journey back to the Old West when the Indian Territory was the most dangerous area for lawmen in the land west of the Mississippi River. Hopefully, as we celebrate and remember outlaws such as Jesse James, Billy the Kid, Butch Cassidy, and the Daltons in western lore, we can now add the name of Cherokee Bill to that list "much feared but highly revered."

Chapter 1

The Legend

On one of my many research trips to Oklahoma during the 1980s, I met a black man near Claremore, who gave me information on Cherokee Bill and his relationship to the black community in eastern Oklahoma. The gentleman told me as a child growing up in the black community, a popular refrain was commonly heard in the early 20th century by blacks. It went like this, *"If I grow up and don't get killed, I want to grow up and be another nigger like Cherokee Bill."*

Most of what originally was known about Cherokee Bill came from the book, *Hell on the Border: He Hanged Eighty-Eight Men*, published in 1898. This book was a 714 page book on Judge Isaac C. Parker and the federal court at Fort Smith, Arkansas, which had jurisdiction over the Indian Territory. At this time in American history, this was the largest federal court in the United States with more than 75,000 square miles within its jurisdiction. Much of what was written about Bill was incorrect, except for the courtroom proceedings, but it did lay the framework for the legend of this outlaw.

Hell on the Border also went into great detail with the significance of the number 13 with Cherokee Bill's life. First, it was thought that he had killed thirteen men during his days on the outlaw path; the reward for the capture of Cherokee Bill was $1300; his first sentence to die was pronounced on April 13; in an attempted jail break, Cherokee Bill killed a jail guard on July 26, or twice thirteen; during that fight

Cherokee Bill—Outlaw

he fired thirteen shots; when Cherokee Bill was convicted, Judge Isaac C. Parker took thirteen minutes in giving the charge to the jury; the actual hours in arriving at a verdict by the jury was thirteen minutes; the jury and deputy during his trial, who ate and slept together made a company of thirteen; and there were thirteen witnesses for the prosecution during Cherokee Bill's trial.

*   *   *   *   *

Although Cherokee Bill was a citizen of the Cherokee Nation in the Indian Territory and is buried in the National Cherokee Cemetery in Fort Gibson, Oklahoma, there hasn't been much acknowledgment of him being a member of the Cherokee Nation. On my visits to the Cherokee National Museum in Tahlequah,Oklahoma, I have not seen him mentioned with other legendary Cherokee outlaws such as Ned Christy or Zeke Procter, both seen as Cherokee patriots today or the Cherokee bank robber, Henry Starr, who was released from prison due to his friendship with Cherokee Bill, more on that later.

The famous Cherokee writer, author and Cherokee Nation historian, Robert J. Conley, recognized Crawford

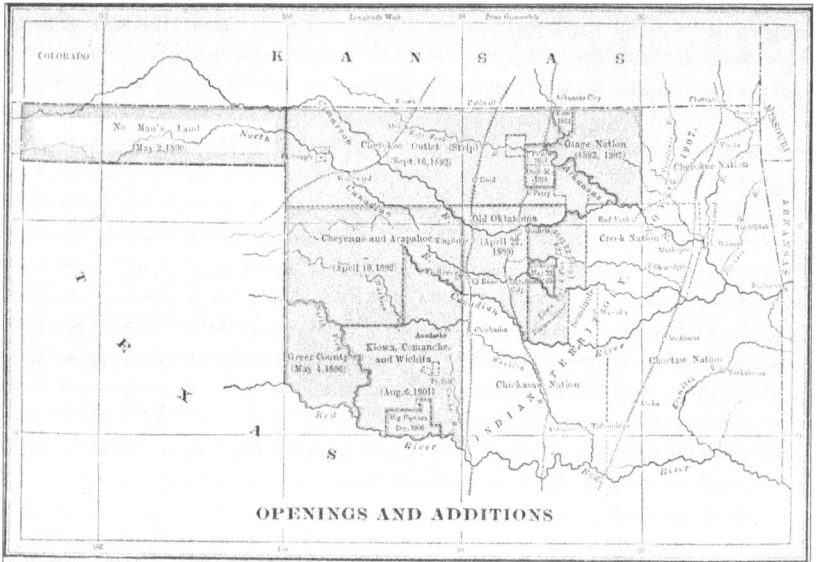

1914 Map of Indian territories and land openings in Oklahoma.

Goldsby as a Cherokee citizen in his writings. In his book, *The Witch of the Goingsnake and Other Stories*, he wrote a short fictional story on Cherokee Bill titled "The Name." Conley also mentioned Cherokee Bill as a Cherokee outlaw in the book *Cherokee* which was a pictorial/historical overview of the Cherokee people in the United States. Conley also included Cherokee Bill in his *A Cherokee Encyclopedia*, which was published by the University of New Mexico Press in 2007.

In 1994, the Cherokee husband and wife team of Jack F. and Anna G. Kilpatrick published a book titled, *Friends of Thunder, Folktales of the Oklahoma Cherokees* that included a section on Cherokee Bill. One of the stories stated ". . . *He robbed just about anything, even a train that was traveling at top speed. Cherokee Bill could do it, and if he had to do it alone, he did it. He even disconnected trains while they were in motion, they say, and when he disconnected one, that left one [coach] on the track, and that's the way he robbed people . . ."*

The noted Oklahoma 'Wild West' historian Glenn Shirley wrote in his book *Toughest of them All*:

> *Take the records of John Wesley Hardin, Bill Longley, Black Jack Ketchum, Sam Bass, or any of the other Western desperadoes, and they can be considered "small potatoes" when compared with Cherokee Bill, the most noted renegade to infest the Oklahoma country in the '90s when "there was no Sunday west of St. Louis, no God west of Fort Smith . . .*
>
> *For more than three years he terrorized this wild country, then known as Indian Territory, and no one cared to attempt to capture him, and at least one town, in the interest of preserving the lives of its citizens, passed an ordinance making it a misdemeanor for anyone to molest him when he was abroad within its limits. Not until a reward of $1,300 was offered for him, dead or alive, did the federal officers begin making plans for his capture . . .*
>
> *In one respect he was a good deal like the modern bandit. He was "a hand with women." He had a sweetheart in nearly every section of the country which he traveled, but the one he loved best was Maggie Glass, the cousin of Ike Rogers, a Cherokee Indian, formerly a deputy United States marshal, and intimately acquainted with the killer.*

During his criminal career, Cherokee Bill was followed by the *New York Times* newspaper giving him unprecedented national attention for an African American criminal at that time in United States history. Some writers have said that Cherokee Bill was only known in a regional context, this is not true. During his time he received national attention. He was also followed by other newspapers around the country, much of it having to do with his association with the Bill Cook gang of the Indian Territory. I will list some of the articles from the *New York Times* later in the text.

Chapter Two

The Family

Much of what is known today of Cherokee Bill's origins was originally published in the book *Hell on the Border* by S. W. Harmon, which was published in 1898. This book focused on the Fort Smith federal court during the Judge Isaac C. Parker reign and the many outlaws and criminals who were captured and executed in that Arkansas federal court and jail. Quite a bit of the book focused on Cherokee Bill because he was the most famous outlaw in the history of the Indian Territory and the Fort Smith federal court. The book stated:

> *Crawford Goldsby was born at Fort Concho, Texas, February 8, 1876, his father being a soldier in the Tenth Cavalry, United States regular army. He was George Goldsby, now a well-to-do and respected farmer, at Cleveland, Oklahoma, where he is known by the name of Bill Scott. He is of Mexican extraction, mixed with white and Sioux Indian. The maiden name of Crawford Goldsby's mother was Ellen Beck, she was half Negro, one-fourth Cherokee Indian and one-fourth white. When he was quite young, Crawford Goldsby's parents separated and until he was seven years old, he lived at Fort Gibson, with his nurse, an old colored aunty, named Amanda Foster . . .*

The birth date and place of origins for Cherokee Bill is correct but clarification on the misinformation above was found in a U.S. army pension request that both George Goldsby and Ellen (Beck) Lynch filed for at different times.

In the pension request interviews, George stated that many times his name was misspelled as Goosbey or Gouldsby. This was because Goldsby was correctly pronounced, in sound, as Gouldsby, not phonetically as Goldsby as most pronounce it today. Additionally, in the interviews, George stated that he lied about his ethnicity because he was married to a white woman. It was common for African American men and women, if they could, to try to pass for another ethnicity in the late 19th century due to the bias and bigotry against black people in this country. Goldsby was especially vulnerable because he was living with a white woman, which could at that time possibly cause serious injury or his death.

*   *   *   *   *

The noted historian and researcher Bennie J. McRae wrote:

> . . . *In a signed deposition on January 29, 1912, George Goldsby stated that he was born in Perry County, Alabama on February 22, 1843. His father was Thornton Goldsby of Selma, Alabama and his mother was Hester King, a mulatto, who resided on her own place west of Summerfield Road between Selma and Marion, George also stated that he had four brothers and two sisters by the same mother and father, Crawford, Abner, Joseph, Blevens, Marie and Susie.*

> *. . . Ellen was born in the Delaware District of the Cherokee Nation, Crawford's maternal grandfather was Luge Beck, described as being a Cherokee of the half blood, and grandmother was Tempy Beck. Both had been slaves once owned by Jeffrey Beck, a Cherokee."*

Amanda Foster, an African American, was also inter-

Cherokee Bill and father George Goldsby.

viewed by the Pension Board in Muskogee, Oklahoma, for Ellen Lynch's request for consideration on February 2, 1912, she was eighty-four years of age at the time. In her interview, Amanda stated that Ellen in her employment with the army waited on the officers at Fort Gibson, she later learned that Ellen and George had married at Fort Sill, Indian Territory. She said that Ellen later came back to Fort Gibson at different times and left four children with her to take care of. Ellen left the boys Crawford, Clarence and the girl Georgia and later the youngest boy Luther. Georgia was the oldest of all the siblings. Amanda said all the children went by the surname of Goldsby. At the time of the interview, Amanda stated that all the children were dead except for Georgia, who married John Foreman and lived near Nowata, Oklahoma. She also said that everyone regarded George as a white man.

Ellen Lynch was interviewed by the pension board on February 3, 1912, she was 53-years-old at the time. She was born in February of 1859 and died December 17, 1932, in Fort Gibson, Oklahoma. Ellen stated that she was at one time the wife of George Goldsby, who afterwards went by the name of William Scott. They were married on July 4, 1874, at Fort Sill, Indian Territory, at the time she was fifteen years of age,

George was twenty-nine.

Ellen stated that she had first met Goldsby at Fort Gibson, Cherokee Nation, in 1872. Goldsby at that time she stated was First Sergeant, Troop H, 10th U.S. Cavalry Regiment, one of the storied Buffalo Soldier units. Ellen went with the troop from Fort Gibson to Fort Sill as the regimental authenticated laundress of D Troop. Once in Fort Sill, Ellen said that Goldsby was transferred to Troop D.

Later, after marriage to Goldsby, but still working as the regimental laundress, the regiment was transferred to Fort Concho near San Angelo, Texas. Ellen stated in the deposition that while at Fort Concho, Goldsby was charged with inciting a riot in San Angelo and a warrant was drawn up for his arrest, which at that time he went AWOL before a trial could take place.

After this occurred, Ellen returned to Fort Gibson, and said George joined her after eight or nine months had elapsed. She said George only stayed in Fort Gibson for a few weeks, after he left, she said she never saw him again. Ellen said the year this took place was 1880.

Evidently, Ellen went back to the 10th U.S. Cavalry Regiment as an "authenticated" laundress. In a later deposition in June of 1923, she stated that after George left her she stayed with the regiment and the government gave her rations, transportation and living quarters wherever the 10th Cavalry was headquartered. Ellen said she was employed at Fort Concho and Fort Davis, Texas, Fort Grant and Fort Apache in Arizona.

According to the 1923 interview, Ellen next married a William Lynch on June 27, 1889, in Kansas City. Lynch was a private in Troop K, 9th U.S. Cavalry Regiment. They met at Fort Apache; Lynch was a ten-year veteran of the regiment

Cherokee Bill and his mother, Ellen.

and later mustered out. They got married in Kansas City, because they stopped there on their way to Fort Gibson. Ellen at this time had served about sixteen years in the employ of the U.S. army.

In the interview with the examiner from the U.S. Pension Board, Ellen stated the following concerning George Goldsby:

. . . I was with him at Fort Concho, Texas and did not go away with him, but he left me there and I stayed there until 1880 when I got money to come back to Fort Gibson. I had four children by George Goldsby. They were Georgia Ellen Goldsby born July 13, 1874 at Fort Sill, I.T.; Crawford J. Goldsby, born at Fort Concho, Texas, February 8, 1876; Clarence Goldsby born at Fort Concho, Texas, September 27, 1877; and Luther Goldsby born at Fort Concho, Texas, August 30, 1879. . . . Goldsby was arrested by the Sheriff? Who went to Seneca, Missouri, and arrested Goldsby and kept him for three weeks waiting for the Texas authorities to come. They did not come and the Sheriff turned him loose and Goldsby went to Eureka Springs, Missouri. . . . Goldsby (George) was cooking at a hotel in Eureka Springs, Arkansas in 1880. . . . He (Goldsby) had

6 children by his next wife before I heard of him again and someone came and told me they saw him somewhere in Kansas. He wrote to the woman (Amanda Foster) who was keeping the children and wanted them to come to Kansas where he could send them to school. . . . He wanted Georgia and Crawford to come. Georgia was 6 or 7, Crawford was between 5 and 6.

Clarence Goldsby

. . . *He (Goldsby) sent a man down after the children and they went to him and the daughter stayed with him until she got married. Crawford and the daughter did not write to me until after the girl, Georgia, was married and they were in the Osage Nation at Hominy or on a farm near there. All of my children are now dead.*

. . . *The way I understand it was not that Goldsby stole a girl and ran off with her to Eureka Springs, Arkansas, but that this girl was a step daughter of the woman that ran the hotel at Eureka where Goldsby was cooking. Amanda Foster went out to Eureka for her health nad when she came back she told me that. The people that kept that hotel were white and I suppose the girl was a white girl.*

. . . *Lynch and I lived together until his death and I buried him. He died in 1916 right in this house where I live now. (Ft. Gibson) . . . I was enrolled on the 1880 Indian rolls as Ellen Beck. I was also enrolled by the Dawes Commission as Ellen Lynch. All of my children were enrolled as Goldsby. No, Crawford was dead, but I applied for enrollment for Luther and Clarence. Georgia was enrolled as the wife of John Foreman. . . .*

In talking more about George Goldsby in her pension interview Ellen said;

I have colored blood in me, and he (Goldsby) always passed as a colored man when I knew him. He said however, that the Pennsylvania Regiment in which he served was a white regiment, and I suppose that he passed as a white man therein . . . I am the mother of "Cherokee Bill," whose correct name was Crawford Goldsby, and the said George Goldsby was his father. The boy was named for George Goldsby's brother. I never saw any of his relatives.

George Goldsby was born on February 22, 1843 in Alabama and died on May 9, 1922 in the Veterans Hospital in Leavenworth, Kansas. George Goldsby in his pension interview in Muskogee, Oklahoma on February 24, 1912 said the following:

. . . I have come to Muskogee and looked you up for the purpose of correcting some false statements I made to you. I have seen Ellen Lynch, what she told you about me being in the service after the Civil War is correct . . . . I changed my name to William Scott on account of that charge against me in Texas. I enlisted in the U.S. Cavalry in September of 1867 and was assigned to Troop G, 10ᵗʰ U.S. Cavalry. . . . I was made first duty-sergeant at first, and was then promoted to Sergeant Major of the regiment in 1872 . . . . I then reenlisted for five years, and was assigned to Troop H,

10th Cavalry. I was shortly made first-orderly sergeant of that troop, and served as such until honorably discharged. . . . I next enlisted in a month or two, in Troop D, 10th U.S. Cavalry for five years, and I served as first-orderly sergeant therein until I deserted at San Angelo, Texas about 1878 or 1879. I was accused of being implicated in a fight or riot down there, and I saw that the race prejudice was so strong, that although I was not guilty of the charge, I deemed it advisable to get away from there. . . . I was with the Quartermaster Department, U.S. Army, just about one year and ten days, there at Harrisburg and Hammelstown, Pennsylvania. . . . I had a half brother [white] by the same father, who was a mail clerk on the road from Montgomery to Selma, Alabama about 1879. . . . My father . . . . died about 1858.

While Sgt. Goldsby was stationed at Fort Concho in West Texas the nearby town of San Angelo proved to be nothing but pure hell for the black troopers. The soldiers on leave would visit the saloon in San Angelo for rest and recreation. When visiting the town the soldiers were harassed, menaced and repeatedly insulted by the white locals. In 1877 and 1878, the black soldiers twice responded to harassment by going to town and shooting up the town saloons where they had been insulted. The second event which involved Sgt. George Goldsby was written about by Frederic Remington in a magazine article in 1901, titled "How the Worm Turned."

The article describing the incident came from an interview Remington had with a black soldier in Cuba during the Spanish-American War, who had been stationed at Fort Concho when the event took place. Sgt. Goldsby was named as the leader of the disgruntled soldiers in the article. Remington also drew a sketch of the soldiers shooting up the saloon. What precipitated the altercation was a black sergeant from Company H, 10th Cavalry Regiment had made a visit to one of the Morris' Saloon in San Angelo, while there a group of white cowboys and hunters had surrounded the sergeant and cut the chevrons from his sleeves, and the stripes from his pants, and had a hearty laugh over the soldiers disposition.

The soldier went back to Fort Concho and told the troops what had happened. Soon thereafter some black soldiers armed with loaded carbines went to Morris' Saloon for retribution. A gunfight took place in which a one white hunter was killed and two others wounded, Private John L. Brown of the 10th Cavalry was killed and another trooper wounded.

Texas Ranger Captain G. W. Arrington showed up later at Fort Concho with a group of rangers with murder warrants for the arrest of First Sergeant George Goldsby and

How the Worm Turns a painting by Frederic Remington painted in 1901 depicting the saloon being shot up by 10th Cavalry troopers.

eight other black troopers involved in the shootout. Goldsby was blamed for allowing the troopers to get their carbines. Colonel Benjamin Grierson, commander of the 10th
Cavalry challenged the authority of the Texas Rangers on a
U.S. army post. It was at this time that Sgt. Goldsby left the
10th Cavalry and went AWOL from military service.

Previous to the 1912 interview, George Goldsby had
been interviewed at Hallett in Pawnee County, Oklahoma,
by a special examiner of the Bureau of Pensions. Goldsby
talked about his family and his service during the Civil War:

*. . . My post office address is R.F.D. #1, Jennings, Pawnee
Co., Okla. . . . I am the identical person who served during
the Civil War in Company "E" 21st, Pennsylvania Volunteer Cavalry, under the name of George Goosby or George
Goosbey. I was enlisted sometime in August 1863, and I
was discharged in June 1865. . . . I was born in Perry Co.,
Alabama. My father was a white man, but my mother was
a mulatto. My mother was Hester King, and my father,
Thornton B. Goldsby of Selma, Ala. My mother lived on
her own place, 4 ½ miles of west of Summerfield, -on the
road to Marion,-Perry Co., Ala. I had brothers, by the same
father and mother, Crawford, Abner, Joseph and Blevens,
and sisters, Mary and Susie. Abner was dead when I returned from the army. Joseph is a preacher in Texas somewhere. Blevens was in Arkansas somewhere years ago.
Crawford died back in Alabama. Susie married and went to
Louisiana, and the last I heard of Mary she was living back
there in Alabama on the old place named above. She married after the war to one James Sanders, who died. She has
a son named James Sanders, also. My mother and father
are both dead. . . . I stayed in Alabama where I was raised*

until May 25, 1863, when I left for Richmond, VA, with a Confederate Company, "D" 8th Alabama, Infantry. I went as a hired servant of the captain, D.C. Perry Nall. . . . Nall came from the Cahaba River there in Alabama. He died on his way from the service. I was servant for him, then, right up until I left them, which was a few days after the battle of Gettysburg, PA. I went immediately to Harrisburg, PA, then, where I engaged as a teamster in the Quarter-Master's Department, U.S. Army, for thirty dollars per month. I was engaged under the name of Goldsby or Goosby, and I remained in such service, there at Harrisburg, until I enlisted in the company and regiment previously named. . . . I was sent to the front to join my company with a bunch of recruits. I joined the company near Petersburg, VA, sometime during the latter part of August, I believe, 1864. We were to the left of Petersburg, and the company was engaged against the defenses around Petersburg. . . .

. . . My company was in the severe engagement during the time. I was with them. The first one was to the left of Petersburg, at what we called Poplar Church. We charged across a field there and captured a fort used in the Petersburg defense. We did not lose many. No one was killed out of our company. I was forced practically to lead the charge, and most of the men should remember this. I pulled Sam Null, who was regarded as a coward, out of the front rank, and I got in his place, as I was in the rear rank. I was stouter, I suppose, and naturally took the lead. Sam Null should remember me pulling him out of the front rank. The Confederates endeavored to take the fort back next day, and lost heavily. We took the fort on August 29, if I recall correctly. We were in the 5th. Army Corps at that time, and were not mounted. Later, we were sent to City Point

and mounted, and transferred to Davies' Brigade, Gregg's Div., Cavalry Corps. We next had a severe engagement on Boynton Plank Road. This was on October 27th. We were in advance of the 2nd, Army Corps, going up to the Plank Road, when we were led into an ambush, a trap, and given a severe pounding. O. C. Bowers was the only man we lost out of the company, however, Lieut. Kendig, it seems to me, was commanding. He was wounded across the breast, while standing behind a post oak tree. I was standing in the road at the time, and he motioned to me to get back out of the road just before he was hit. He received only a slight wound. . . . We were then engaged tearing up the Weldon Railroad, and a raid towards Belleville, North Carolina. We were then detailed as body-guard for General Wright, who commanded the 6th, Army Corps, and had headquarters at the "Yellow House," on the Weldon R.R., 18 miles south of Petersburg. We were there, then, from December 1864 to about April 1865. We were at the Surrender of Lee, and then went into Washington, and took part in the Grand Review. I was discharged there in Washington, as I had only enlisted for one year. The company went on to Lynchburg, VA, then to Harrisburg, PA, where they were mustered out.

The information Goldsby gave was quite illuminating, here was a black man that entered the Civil War as a paid servant for the Confederate army. During the Battle of Gettysburg, he went over to the Union side and joined the U.S. army. Most blacks in the U.S. army served in segregated units, but George was one of the African Americans who were light skinned enough or could pass and didn't raise any concerns to serve in white units during the war. In the white Pennsylvania cavalry regiment, George was able to attain the rank of corporal in unit. The Battle of Petersburg was one of the major conflicts during the Civil War. George served with valor in the heat of battle and was able to take part in the Grand Review in Washington, D.C., which segregated black units were not allowed to do at the end of the war. Goldsby was a Civil War veteran of distinction.

Goldsby continued his interview with what happened after the war:

> . . . I was always called "George" by my family in Alabama. I went back there were I was raised in December 1865, and I stayed about one year. . . . I haven't been back there to Alabama except once since. . . . They tried to lynch me in there at that time, and I haven't been back since. . . . The two Smiths that I named saw me with my company at Appomattox Court House, VA, at the time of the surrender. . . . That was why they threatened to lynch me back there, because I had left the company, the Confederate company, and had enlisted in the Union Army. . . .

The special examiner for the Bureau of Pensions, Department of the Interior named Bowie wrote the following notes on Goldsby in regards to his interview on February 26, 1912:

> . . . This claimant served during the Civil War in a company of white soldiers, evidently representing himself therein as a white man. He admits his mother was a mulatto, and that he was born in the plantation section of Alabama, his father having been his mother's former owner. She was evidently, from what the claimant states, freed by this owner. Claimant could readily pass for a white man, and, in fact, his present wife is a white woman, and his children by this woman all associate with white persons, and are regarded

as of white blood. It is evidently believed by some in the community where claimant now lives that he has some colored blood in him, as he was referred to by some as "Nigger" Scott, however, I could see that acquaintances did not know what to really believe about it. Claimant's former wife, now Ellen Lynch . . . ., is a mixture of Cherokee Indian, Negro and white blood, and her present husband is a Negro. Claimant passed as a Negro in the Tenth Cavalry, and this was one of his reasons, I suppose, for concealing his service in the Tenth Cavalry. Claimant had a son by his former wife, Crawford Goldsby, who was one of the most noted outlaws and desperadoes in the history of the Indian Territory. He was commonly known as "Cherokee Bill," and was hanged at Ft. Smith, Ark. in 1896. "Hell on the Border" is the title of a book containing the history of those days. I learned, incidentally, while in the vicinity of claimant's home that the claimant was the father of "Cherokee Bill," and he apparently reluctantly admitted the fact. . . . He [Goldsby] admitted to me that the true reason why this wife and he was married in Kansas, after having been married by ceremony in Arkansas, was that his wife's step-father found out that he had colored blood in him, and the laws of Arkansas prohibited the inter-marriage of persons of Negro and white blood. The laws of Kansas, he stated, did not contain such a provision. . . .

. . . Claimant told me that the author of the book named above had made an error in stating that he was of Mexican and Sioux Indian extraction. Doubtless claimant so advised him, however, to explain his very dark complexion, due to the Negro blood in him. . . .

Now we know where the earlier reports of Cherokee Bill

being part Mexican and Sioux Indian come from. George Goldsby was not trying to gain a pension for his service with the all black 10th U.S. Cavalry Regiment, he had petitioned for a pension with his service with the white 21st Pennsylvania Volunteer Cavalry Regiment during the Civil War. He was successful in gaining a pension for his Civil War service. After his death, both of his wives continued to petition the Pension Board as widows of a veteran. Goldsby never officially divorced his black first wife, Ellen Beck (Lynch), so the government decided to give her a pension and his white second wife's petition was dismissed, since her marriage was deemed not legal.

The second wife in my estimation gave the most illuminating testimony during all the pension interviews. Her maiden name was Effie Amanda Henshaw, after marrying Goldsby, she went by the last name of Scott. She was interviewed in Pawnee County, Oklahoma, on July 24, 1923. Effie was born on September 7, 1864, in Chicago, Illinois, and her mother died when she was four-years-old. She lived in St. Louis, Missouri, for a while, and then moved to Eureka Springs, Arkansas, in 1880 to live with her father.

Effie's father ran a hotel in town called The St. Louis Hotel, which later burned down. Effie met George in the fall of 1881 at the hotel, where he had gained employment as a cook. After running away, they got married on Thanksgiving Day of 1881. She was seventeen years of age, George was thirty-eight. A black preacher named McGee married them and they moved to Columbus, Kansas. From there they lived in Pittsburg, Girard, Cherokee, and finally Cherryvale, Kansas. Effie said that they went through another marriage ceremony at Cherryvale on April 15, 1886, at the request of her grandfather.

George married this time under the name of Goldsby, but still went by the name of William Scott. The reason for the move to Cherryvale was to allow George to get work with the Atchison, Topeka and Santa Fe Railroad. They later moved to Guthrie, Oklahoma Territory, and then to Arkansas City and Wichita in Kansas. Effie stated that they also lived six years in the Osage Nation, Indian Territory, to 1898, then moved to Pawnee County, Oklahoma Territory. Effie and George had six children from their marriage.

Effie stated in her interview with the Pension Board:

. . . A letter from the woman [Ellen Lynch] came to me asking about a divorce. I talked to Goldsby and he said he did not see why he should be mixed up in such a thing as he was not married to the woman and therefore did not need any divorce. . . . I have no evidence . . . to any divorce. . . . Goldsby and I had always lived together as man and wife from the time of marriage to time of his death, but shortly before his death he had gone to the Soldier's Home and died the second day after his admission.

Later Effie wrote a letter to the Pension Board on January 28, 1924 where she talked about the Goldsby family:

. . . His (Russian) grandmother after several years located his mother in Alabama and obtained her freedom and made her home with her daughter on the [Thornton] Boykin Goldsby plantation, [Thornton] Boykin Goldsby (this was the soldier's father) owned more than "three hundred slaves," among them were several bright women he used as concubines, so it was natural that he had a number of kin people of African descent, the same as a great many of the South. I will enclose a lock of his hair and if you can detect any trace of the Negro in it would you let me know. . . .

Thornton Boykin Goldsby

Clarence came to our house in the year of 1903 as he supposed to see his father. Mr. Scott told him he was not his father. Georgie [Georgia] looked like a quadroon while Crawford looked more like a mulatto and had kinky hair. Clarence was still darker than Crawford, a very dark brown, almost black. I couldn't tell what his hair was like as he had it shaved close to his head. Luther came to our house also and he was lighter than any of them and his hair was also cut close. Now I had the care of Georgia and Crawford from the time they were nine and seven till they were fifteen. Mrs. Amanda Foster wrote to Mr. Scott in 1883 telling him she could not keep them any longer, and he sent for Georgia and Crawford. He always said the other two were not his, and he couldn't swear that Crawford was his, "Before Crawford was a month old, Ellen was out all day riding with a Negro private." I have heard the names of five . . . men that she had been with, but I cannot remember them, but it seems that after she married Lynch, she settled down and lived a respectable life.

. . . When Crawford was in jail in Ft. Smith, she hired

lawyer Reed to defend him at our expense, telling him that we were well off, right there, I was bare-footed and only rags for clothing, and my children the same. . . .

Effie was very familiar with all of George's children by Ellen; it is interesting that George didn't claim the two youngest boys that used his last name. Crawford and his sister lived a number of years with their father and step-mother in Kansas. Earlier accounts of Crawford attending Catholic Indian School in Carlisle, Pennsylvania, are not documentable. He probably attended school in Cherokee, Kansas, while living with his father. There is no evidence of an Indian school in Cherokee, Kansas.

Chapter Three

Young Crawford Goldsby

When Crawford reached the age of twelve, he came to his mother's home in Fort Gibson, Cherokee Nation, Indian Territory. He found his mother had married William Lynch a local barber who owned a barbershop in Fort Gibson for many years. Crawford and Lynch didn't get along and he began lying out and associating with the worst of companions, developing a taste for liquor and rebelling against authority.

At the age of fifteen, Crawford left Fort Gibson and went to live with his older sister, Georgia. She had married her first husband named Mose Brown and lived near Nowata, Cherokee Nation, on claims gained by her mother's Cherokee Freedman status. Mose took a dislike to Crawford and continually mistreated him to the extent that Crawford left and returned to Fort Gibson. In Fort Gibson, Crawford made his home with a Cherokee Freedman by the name of Bud Buffington.

Cherokee did odd jobs by the time he was seventeen. Alex R. Matheson, a shopkeeper in Fort Gibson, in an interview said, "He cleaned up and swept out our store. He was the best working, the most honest Negro boy that worked for us."

On another occasion before he got in trouble with the law, Crawford worked as a cowboy on a small cattle ranch owned by James W. Turley and his father. In the *Indian Pio-*

Fort Gibson *circa* 1899

neer Papers, James W. Turley gave the following comments concerning Crawford:

> . . . *One day when they were breaking a young colt, Jim's father got the rope tangled about his wrist and was dragged by the colt, and his wrist joint was dislocated. On this account, Jim hired a young colored boy, who came up to their place looking for work. This boy wearing a ragged cap, was bare footed, and coatless, and said his name was Crawdford Goldsby.*
>
> *In the fall when Jim got a job at Halsell's ranch on Bird Creek, this colored boy stayed with Jim's father and did the chores for his room and board. In the spring he was paid wages for his work. That summer, he wanted a horse and saddle to go to Fort Gibson to see his mother. The Turley's gave him the saddle, and Jack Johnson furnished the horse.*
>
> *Crawford was gone about three weeks, but came back with the horse and saddle. He asked Jim for advice on what to do about his killing a man at Fort Gibson and Jim advised him to go back and give himself up to the marshal.*

Crawford did this, and in about three weeks was back again with the Cook gang. . . .

Before Crawford got into trouble at Fort Gibson, he was a quiet, good-natured, hard-working, boy, well-liked by all who knew him. At one time he rode up to where Jim and his father were walling up a well, got off his horse, and said to Jim, "You know you are liable to get shot?" Crawford said, "I haven't got it in for you, I'd rather shoot anyone else than you. Your father is all right down in the well. There are posses over at the house, looking for me, and there is liable to be a shooting match here. If I could see to pick out Heck Bruner, I'd like to get him.

He stood there motionless, and unafraid with his eyes on the Deputies and their posses, until they left the house, and crossed Flat Rock Creek, and were out of sight on their way toward Tulsa, whereupon he turned and asked Jim for food. Jim told him that he or anyone else was welcome to eat at the Turley home, so Cherokee Kid got himself a sandwich and rode off toward the North, eating as he rode. The next and last time that Crawford Goldsby was ever seen by Jim Turley was at Fort Smith, Arkansas, when the hangman was preparing to end the life of Cherokee Bill on the gallows."

Turley stated in the interview that Crawford gave himself up to the marshal on his advice, but there is no evidence this ever happened. Most evidence points to the contrary.

Crawford's first run-in with the law occurred during his eighteenth year, in the early spring of 1894. One night while attending a dance in the African American area of Fort Gibson called "old town," he and Jake Lewis, an older black Cherokee tough had a confrontation over his younger brother, Clarence. While trying to protect his younger brother, Crawford was severely beaten by Lewis and his friends.

The next day, Crawford caught up with Lewis in a stable in Fort Gibson and shot him twice with a pistol. Crawford left him for dead, mounted a horse and rode deep into the Cherokee Nation. Alex R. Matheson who worked at the F. H. Nash Mercantile Store in Fort Gibson talked about Cherokee Bill's mishap in Fort Gibson:

> . . . *About the only trouble he had was a few fist fights until one nigh he went to a dance and had a fight with a Negro boy by the name of Bill [Jake] Lewis. A Negro deputy sheriff was there and held his gun on Cherokee Bill while Lewis beat him up. Lewis worked for Mr. Bowden on Garrison Hill. Early the next morning, Cherokee Bill went to the Bowden barn and hid in a manger and waited until Lewis showed up. When Lewis was inside the barn, Cherokee Bill stepped out of the manger and shot Lewis three or four times but did not kill him. Although he was shot up pretty bad, as Cherokee Bill was using a .45 six shooter, I lived about two blocks from the Bowden home. After the shooting, Cherokee Bill went from the Bowden home to Frenchy Miller's, a distance of about a quarter of a mile, as none of them were up he went to the barn and saddled up one of the Miller's horses and rode to where the Cook Gang was holed up on Fourteen Mile Creek; about where the town of Hulbert is now located, and joined the gang. That was the beginning of his outlaw career. . .*

The authorities in the Cherokee Nation put out an attempted murder warrant on Goldsby. Being that both parties were citizens of the Cherokee Nation there was no federal warrant for Goldsby. All the Five Civilized Tribes

Indian nations in the Indian Territory had their own judges, police and courts in the Indian Territory.

Lewis was seriously wounded but recovered from the gunshot wounds. Crawford took up with Bill Cook whom he had met earlier while working together as cowboys, and Jim Cook, both mixed-blood Cherokee. A mixed-blood in the Indian Territory was

Bill Cook

a person with Indian and European ancestry. Bill Cook previously had served as a posse man for Deputy U.S. Marshal Bill Smith, a mixed-blood Delaware Indian. Smith would later play a major role in the capture of Cherokee Bill. When Crawford joined up with the Cook brothers, there was a decision made that they would follow the trail of the outlaw. Bill Cook was designated to be the leader of the gang, which now became known as the Bill Cook gang.

The United States government purchased from the Cherokee Nation an area known as the Cherokee Outlet, which consisted of 6.5 million acres of land, located on the northwest edge of the Indian Territory. This outlet is sometimes erroneously called the Cherokee Strip, which was in Kansas. In 1893, the Cherokees received $8.5 million, of which each person on the tribal roll received an initial payment of $265.68. Payments were made to citizens at selected towns.

The administrator of payment was E. E. Starr, treasurer of the Cherokee Nation.

In June of 1894, at Tahlequah in the Cherokee Nation, Bill and Jim Cook requested their share of the land payment. Effie Crittenden, a good friend, agreed to pick up their share when she got hers, they were leery of the lawmen in the area. Bill and Jim convinced Goldsby that she could be trusted and gave her written request for all three of their money portions to the Cherokee treasurer. Mrs. Crittenden was the manager of the Half-Way House, a stagecoach stop fourteen miles west of Tahlequah.

The Cook brothers had a sister, who was married to Bob Harden, the cook of the Half-Way House. Mrs. Crittenden was separated from her husband, Richard "Dick" Crittenden, a Cherokee policeman, he and his brother, E. C. "Zeke," earlier both had served as deputy U.S. marshals, they lived near Wagoner, Creek Nation.

On June 15, Mrs. Crittenden went to Tahlequah, her estranged husband who was a guard for the payment and read the names on the request she gave the treasurer. Crittenden knew that two of the men had outstanding Cherokee warrants, Crawford Goldsy for attempted murder, and Bill Cook for larceny was waiting at the Half-Way House.

Crittenden proceeded to tell Sheriff Leonard Williams of the Tahlequah District, what he had learned. Deputy Sheriff Ellis Rattling Gourd led a ten-man Indian police posse to bring in the young outlaws. The other men in the posse were Sequoyah Houston, Bill Bracket, Bill McKee, Isaac Grease, George Parris, Bob Woodall, Nelson Hicks, and brothers E. C. "Zeke" and Dick Crittenden.

Of the posse members, Houston was the most striking, he was a full blood, tall and handsome with a mustache.

He was thirty-two years of age, father of four and was from Blue Springs, then known as Gideon in the Cherokee Nation. Houston had spent five years with the Cherokee police, was an excellent shot with a pistol and Winchester. He had captured many horse thieves that rode the open range of that Indian Nation. Houston always wore a wide flat-brimmed hat and rode a white horse, he had told his wife he would come home that night as soon as his mission was completed.

The payment was closed on Saturday, June 16, in Tahlequah with the next stop being in the town of Vinita. Gourd and his posse left the Tahlequah courthouse at noon, Sunday, June 17, and reached Fourteen Mile Creek at sundown. The posse found out before it got to Fourteen Mile Creek that the stagecoach from Tahlequah had been robbed by four men and they sent two of the posse back to Tahlequah for more reinforcements.

The stagecoach station was a log structure with a smokehouse and a barn in the back, stood in a tree grove on the west back facing the creek. Goldsby and the Cooks, through the efforts of Effie Crittenden, had received their pay on the last day of the treasurer's stay in Tahlequah. Sheriff Gourd and the posse had followed Effie at a distance back to the house with the intention of capturing the outlaws.

Goldsby and the Cooks had planned on leaving the vicinity the next night on Monday, July, 18. On Sunday evening, Goldsby was outside sitting under a tree when he sighted riders below the ridge and recognized the white horse of Houston. Goldsby grabbed his rifle and dashed inside and gave the warning to prepare for a fight.

The posse rode up quickly and Rattling Gourd called out, "We have you boys surrounded, you might as well give up!"

Goldsby shouted back, "We will never do it, but we'll swap out with you!"

An intense gunfight followed, sadly, Sequoyah Houston was killed by a shot from Goldsby's Winchester. After Houston fell Rattling Gourd and four of his posse fled, leaving the Crittendens to face the danger. The brothers knew they were in a bad spot, but decided to fight it out until they were able to escape in the dark.

The Crittendens took cover in the smoke house during the gunfight, Goldsby and Bill Cook made a dash for their horses in the barn while shooting at the lawmen. Dick Crittenden was able to wound Jim Cook with his shotgun. Jim was able to retrieve his Winchester and covered his brother and Goldsby with gunfire. Jim couldn't reach his horse so he jumped up behind his brother on his horse. The young outlaws were able to escape into the darkness.

Later a much larger posse arrived at the Half-Way House after news of Houston's death reached Tahlequah. Bob Harden, the Cook's brother-in-law, was taken into custody, but later released by authorities in Fort Smith after a hearing. Effie Crittenden was interviewed and asked directly if Crawford Goldsby had been in the fight. She replied, "No it was not Crawford Goldsby, but it was Cherokee Bill." Crawford was previously known by this nickname, but after this incident he was forever known by everyone as "Cherokee Bill." Even his mother, Ellen Lynch, called him "Cherokee Bill."

Bill Cook had intentions of getting a doctor for his brother at Fort Gibson, they knew they were being pursued by a large posse. Cook and Cherokee Bill located a doctor named Howard in Fort Gibson and forced him to attend to Jim

Cook's wounds, then they threatened his life if he talked to anyone. They quickly stole another horse and rode west toward the junctions of the Arkansas and Grand Rivers. They were able to ferry across the Arkansas River on Tuesday, June 19 into the Creek Nation.

The *Muskogee Phoenix* newspaper on June 21, gave a report on how Jim Cook was captured by lawmen. Deputy U.S. Marshal John B. McGill went down to the ferry on the Arkansas River to get on the trail of the outlaws. He was told the outlaws were resting at a family home named Capps near the ferry. It was reported that three outlaws were seen at the Capps' house, but only two left.

McGill found Jim Cook's Winchester rifle and horse and a watch which was identified as the one taken from a store at Springfield when it was robbed recently. Jim Cook was not in the house but had crawled down to the river and was hiding in a ravine.

The deputy located Cherokee Bill and Bill Cook in a pasture owned by a Mr. Cobb, near the Capps' farm, and sent immediately for help from Muskogee. McGill was able to sneak up on their horses and take one while Cherokee Bill and Cook were hiding in the brush. The outlaws shot at McGill as he made off with the horse.

Goldsby mounted the remaining horse and gave chase to McGill who rode up to a home on the Cobb place, dismounted and hitched the horse beside his own. He ran into the nearby stable and started shooting at Cherokee Bill, who in turn was firing shots from horseback with his Winchester at McGill. A lady at the farm house said Bill fired eleven shots at the deputy. The outlaw was very close to McGill when the posse from Muskogee arrived on the scene, slyly Cherokee Bill and Bill Cook were able to elude the posse and get away.

The posse from Muskogee was able to capture Jim Cook in his hiding spot near the river. He surrendered without putting up a fight and was taken to the federal jail in Muskogee.

In the *Indian Pioneer Papers* at the Oklahoma Historical Society, John Hannon an early white resident of the Creek Nation in the 1930s gave an interview of what happened to Cherokee Bill and Bill Cook during the fight outside Muskogee:

> *. . . Bill Cook and Cherokee Bill went up on top of Kaler Hill, unsaddled their horses, stretched some blankets up on some poles for a shade, and lay down to rest while their horses grazed and rested. Pretty soon a Deputy U.S. Marshal came and spied them up there. Cherokee Bill's horse had grazed off down the hillside quite a way from them. The marshal crawled in the grass up to the horse and got him started to a house where a man named Addington lived. Before he got there, though, Bill saw him, grabbed his Winchester and started after him. The marshal ran in and told Addington what was up and deputized him to help him. Mr. Addington's folks were sick so he said, "We can't fight here, let's go to the barn." They slipped out and got behind the barn, and as Bill came by, the marshal commanded him to put up his hands. Bill dropped to one knee, fired several shots into the corner of the barn, right at them, then ran for his horse. The marshal, instead of shooting him, shot the horse. When Bill saw the horse fall, he turned and went after the marshal who fled. Cherokee Bill and Bill Cook then got the other horse, went down to a farm house, took a horse and rode on.*

Burl Taylor, a black man, who was a citizen of the Creek Nation, had several encounters with Cherokee Bill, he gave another version of what he witnessed after the Fourteen Mile Creek fight:

> While I was working at the Nevins ferry, my horse strayed and I was out looking for it. I met Bob Elliott just west of Telephone ferry. He asked me where I was going, I told him I was looking for my horse; he then asked me to go with him and warn Cherokee Bill and Bill Cook that Bill Stout had gone to Muskogee to tell the U.S. marshal where they were hiding and he would help me find my horse. I asked him where they were hid and he pointed upon the hill where the school for the blind is located. And said, "See where those yellow slickers are spread over the bushes for shade? Well they are under them." We started in behind Bill Stout, when he got just north of the hill we turned south up the hill to where Cherokee and Bill were. When we arrived, Cherokee said, "Come on under and cool off." Bob Elliot answered, "We don't have time." Then said, "See Bill Stout going yonder." Bill Cook answered, "Yes." Bob told him that Stout was on his way to Muskogee to tell the marshal where they were hiding. Cherokee said he could not believe it, every time he and Bill made a good haul, they always gave Stout a hand full of money and gave his wife a lot of money to cook meals for them.
>
> Pretty soon we saw a dust cloud coming from Musk-ogee, it was not long until we counted thirteen in the marshal's posse. Bob and I went south across the hill after we got about even with the old Will Robinson place; Bob stopped and said, "Let's wait here and see the fun." The posse went on around the hill to Will Robinson's place and hid in the crib and barn. They told Mr. Robinson and

his wife to go across the road to the Madden home so they would not get hurt. Cherokee and Bill Cook rode down toward the crib, a man in the crib fired at Cherokee and killed his horse. Cherokee grabbed his Winchester and stood up where his horse was shot, firing at the officers. Cook kept telling him to come on and they would get another horse; Cherokee answered that he would go as soon as he finished the round of shells in the Winchester. After he finished firing, he got on the horse behind Cook; they started south at a fast gait and Cherokee lost his hat in the strong wind. He jumped off the horse and started back for it. He had his Winchester gripped in both hands, raised over his head. He was running as fast as he could, letting out a loud whoopie and curses each step. The posse thought he was coming back after them, they all jumped on their horses and ran for it. Cherokee had a big laugh over it, they went on toward Coody Creek and met a man driving a horse and buggy.

Cherokee got off and taken the man's horse from the buggy and went back and got his saddle. Just a few days before this Jim Cook was captured at Bill Stout's place on the river. Jim had been wounded a few days before he was captured, he saw the officers coming and run from the house and hid in the brush. The officers combed the brush until they found him. I taken them across the river as they took him to the Fort Smith jail. They had to turn him free at Fort Smith because what he was charged with was not a federal offense and happened in the Cherokee Nation. That night Cherokee and Bill came to Muskogee and went to Captain Sever's place, located about where the Severs' hotel is now located. They then went to the barn and got two sorrel horses that belonged to Captain Severs. They were fine horses. They then went to the Stout home on the river to kill Bill Stout, but Bill was hiding out. They made several trips there looking for him. One night they slipped into the chicken coop and stayed all night but Bill never showed up.

Chapter Four

Cherokee Bill Outlaw

By the summer of 1894, Cherokee Bill was eighteen years old and stood right at six feet tall. He was a burly, broad-shouldered man possessing great physical strength. His features were distinctly African, including thick lips and kinky black hair. He was asked once what was his ethnicity, he replied, "I am one half white, one half Indian and one half Negro."

With his Winchester rifle he could burst a squirrel eye as far as he could see—every shot—and he said that he could shoot from his waist on a level and hardly ever miss his target. It was said for target practice; Cherokee Bill along with his buddies would ride out into the territory prairie and find a secluded location where he then mounted his horse and galloped at full speed around a tree that had a paper target nailed on it. Circling the tree he would hit the target dead center riding at full speed on each pass while firing his Winchester rifle.

Residents of the Indian Territory who knew him best said Cherokee Bill would take long journeys through the woods and that his mental alertness during his sleepless night while playing the game with his shrewd foes left him almost limp, silent, morose. He would talk in monosyllables and would get on the move again. When he rode into any town, he would plunge into wild, lawless acts and spend very freely the "hot money" for drinking and gambling. In such company as he was in most of the time, fights were common. He never seemed to be afraid of anyone or anything.

Cherokee Bill

People in the territory said that Cherokee Bill favored wearing large flat brim white hats with a large red band and a small feather. Around his neck he wore a very large bandana, on his boots he wore Mexican jingle bob spurs and he wore fancy leather chaps that were metal studded. You can say he was a flamboyant outlaw cowboy.

Not long after the Fourteen Mile Creek fight, the famous Cook Gang was organized, with Cherokee Bill as a co-leader, along with Bill Cook. The gang was made up of white, black and Indian men. The gang would change in size over the months, but the original members recruited for the gang were Lon Gordon,

George Sanders, and
Henry Munson, black
men from the Indian
Territory. It was said
that Sanders was the
brother of Levi Sanders,
who had robbed the
Fort Gibson stagecoach
and was killed during
the Indian payment at
Tahlequah.

Sam "Verdigris
Kid" McWilliams, Cur-
tis "Curt" Dayson, Jess
"Buck" Snyder, and El-
mer "Chicken" Lucas
were white men. Jim
French and Bill Cook

Jim French—Outlaw

were Cherokee mix-bloods, French was from Fort Gibson,
where his Cherokee father operated a ferry on Grand River
until his death in 1890, and his mother was a white woman. French was being sought on a federal warrant issued on
September 13, 1893, for robbery of the U.S. mail in the Indian Territory when he joined the Cook gang. So this was the
origins of the gang that would become a household name in
the Indian Territory. The only gang to gain more notoriety
in the Indian Territory was the Dalton Gang of earlier fame.

The gang would not always operate as one unit, but
work in pairs, trios, and sextets. At different points in time,
other outlaws would join them in their escapades. The gang
not only became big in the local press, but developed a national following with their daring do of various crimes in

the Indian Territory. They were referred to in the press as the "The Cook Gang" with Cherokee Bill taking great prominence in the reporting.

On July 2, 1894, in the afternoon, two riders rode into the small Creek Nation town of Wetumka below the North Fork of the Canadian River. The two riders got off their horses in front of Scales Mercantile Store. Upon entering the store, they produced pistols and proceeded to rob the establishment. They took a sack of money headed north across the river. The robbers were said to have been Cherokee Bill and Jim French, riding hell bent for leather.

On July 5, at approximately ten o'clock, Dick Richards, station agent for the Kansas-Arkansas Valley Railroad at Nowata was waiting for the north bound train on the platform during a usual quiet night. He was startled with the command to "Throw up your hands." Richards was confronted by two people he didn't know, black outlaws, Cherokee Bill and Henry Munson, with pistols drawn. Richards made a big mistake, he went for his pistol, Cherokee Bill immediately shot him fatally with a wound to the neck. The shot woke up the town and Bill and Munson fled into the night.

The townspeople laid Richards' body in the waiting room of the train station. There was a bullet burn along the forefinger of his left gun hand, which demonstrated he had a bead on the robbers but was too slow to pull the trigger. Richards left a wife and two small children. On July 6, 1894, the Guthrie *Oklahoma State Capital* newspaper said, ". . . . *Cherokee Bill is the fiercest of the Cook gang. . . . Should he be killed the band would go to pieces.*"

The same morning the previous newspaper article came out concerning Cherokee Bill, the paper carried another article that stated at 9 a.m., six masked highway men held up the stagecoach that ran between Fort Gibson and Muskogee. The bandits stopped the stage one mile east of the Arkansas River. The passengers on the stage were Joshua Ross, superintendent of the Cherokee Male Seminary at Tahlequah; J. W. Singleton, manager of the Phoenix Printing Company and a salesman named Norris, all of whom were relieved of their money and valuables.

Seeing how the bandits were wearing mask no identification could be made, but it was assumed it was the Cook Gang. Another crime that was laid at the feet of the Cook Gang was the murder and robbery of a man from Muldrow of $1000. The alert was given all over the Cherokee and Creek Nations to be on the lookout for the Cook Gang, and posses, federal and Indian was in the field searching.

The next opportunity for the Cook gang came on July 18, when Bill Cook was informed about a large sum of money was coming to the Red Fork train station on the Frisco Railroad as payment for a shipment of cattle from the Spike S Ranch. The gang devised a plan for the robbery that consisted of Elmer Lucas holding the horses for the gang during the robbery; he was nicknamed "Chicken" that day because he was fearful of the robbery.

The outlaws took over the station before the train arrived and took charge of the station agent. Cherokee Bill, Bill Cook, Lonnie Gordon, Sam McWilliams, Henry Munson and Curtis Dayson broke in and ransacked the building looking for cash. After the train stopped at the station; Dayson, Munson and Baldwin captured the engine crew at gunpoint. Cherokee Bill and Cook were in charge of robbing the express car where the money should have been. They searched the car for forty-five minutes and only found fifteen dollars, a jug of good whiskey, and a box of cigars. The station agent had hid the money in receipt book and dropped it on the platform during the robbery. He retrieved it later after the gang was satisfied that no money was on the train. The station agent asked if he could get his receipt book and the gang said sure they didn't want a book. The gang allowed the train to leave for Sapulpa the next stop and rode off.

Other African Americans who later rode with the Cook Gang included the notorious train robbing outlaws Creek Freedman Buss Luckey and Cherokee Freedman Tom Root.

Chapter Five

The Bank Robbery

The boldest and most brazen robbery by Cherokee Bill and the Cook Gang occurred on Monday morning, July 30, 1894. That was the day the gang robbed the Lincoln County Bank in Chandler, Oklahoma Territory. Chandler was the county seat of Lincoln County; a few years later, the famous Dodge City, Kansas, lawman Bill Tilghman would become sheriff of Lincoln County.

At about ten o'clock on that July morning, five heavily armed cowboys rode into town from the northeast, coming down Manvel Avenue to 7th Street, where they turned and went to the alley. They rode behind Fletcher's Hardware Store and stopped at the rear of the Lincoln County Bank, where they dismounted. The *Chandler News* newspaper on August 3, 1894, described what happened then:

> . . . *Reports differ as to the number of men in the gang, bit in generally agreed that there were five in the company from the north. When they were opposite the rear of the bank, they turned in and rode to the back of the building where they dismounted. It is said that a sixth man came up the alley from the south and joined them here. Three of the men went to the front of the building, passing around the small building at the south of the bank. One stopped on the sidewalk in front of the bank, and the other two entered, covering J. H. Kee, the president of the bank, and O. B. Kee, the cashier, with their guns, and commanding them to*

throw up their hands. Mrs. J. H. Kee and Mrs. O. B. Kee, who were in the building when the robbers entered rushed out through the back door, passing one of the robbers who was entering.

One of the men went to the back room, where F. B. Hoyt, the assistant cashier was sick in bad, and dragged him into the bank, ordering him to open the safe. It so happened, however, that when the safe had been opened at the opening of the bank, the cashier had taken out what money he wanted and turned on the time-lock, so that it was impossible to open the safe. Some $300 was on the counter, but in their haste the robbers overlooked the greater portion of it and took only $107.50.

. . . J. B. Mitchell was sitting in front of his barber shop nearly opposite the bank, and when he realized what was going on he began to cry "the Daltons are in town," and "they're robbing the bank." One of the robbers in front of the bank called to him to shut up, and just as he rose from his chair the robber shot him, the ball entering his right side below and to the rear of the arm pit. Mr. Mitchell staggered a few feet and sank to the sidewalk near the corner of his shop, where he died in about two minutes. Shots were fired at several other persons, but no one was hit.

W. N. Warren, who was in his house half a block south of the bank when the firing began, started down the alley for his gun, and was shot at several times by one of the gang in the rear of the bank. When he returned he fired from his kitchen window and killed one of the horses. He fired several other shots, and as Geo. Strode and Arthur Ellis were also firing, it is likely that some of the shots took effect. When the robbers came out of the bank they mounted their *horses, two on one o the horses and rode out as they came in. Sheriff Parker was the first in pursuit, following them to the north end of town, firing as they went, and there he got of his horse and shot at them till they were out of sight. How many of the shots took effect is not known, but Parker killed another of their horses here. At Mr. Pollard's in the northeast part of town, they took a horse that was standing there with a saddle on, to replace the one killed at the bank. After they turned north by the Bullard farm they met an old German in a cart and stopped him, cut the horse loose and rode him off. Sheriff Parker, W. N. Warren, Joe Orr, Paul Hunter, Arthur Hillis and Mont Bevins followed closely after the retreating robbers.*

. . . After crossing the Chuckahoe, Sheriff Parker's posse came in sight of the gang, and followed them into the timber, where they seemed to scatter. It was here that a loose horse was found and a little later, one of the robbers was surrounded and taken. The man had been wounded, a ball having passed through both thighs; but whether he was shot before he left town or while being captured is not definitely known: probably the former. The wounded man was brought back to town and Paul Hunter and Mont Bevins followed the trail of one robber to the Agency, reaching that place about an hour after he passed through. Being unable to secure a posse and fresh horses they returned to town.

The *Guthrie Daily Leader* earlier on August 1, 1894 carried a front page story that said:

DASTARDLY DEED OF DEMONS.
THE LINCOLN COUNTY BANK AT CHANDLER LOOTED.
A CITIZEN RUTHLESSLY SLAIN.
Sheriff Parker and Posse Give Chase. A Terrific Battle

and as Outlaw Brought Town – Now Safe Behind the Bars. A Mere Boy is He but the Others are Old Timers – Latest Job of the Notorious Cook Gang.

Special to the Leader.

Chandler, Ok., July 31. – *The quiet and serenity of this little city was rudely disturbed yesterday morning by a bold bank robbery. About 9 o'clock, five horsemen dressed as typical cowboys and heavily armed, rode into town from the north along the street east of the court house, and turning down the alley back of Fletcher's hardware store, proceeded to the rear of the Lincoln County Bank where they dismounted.*

One of the men held the horses while two entered the building from the rear and one from the front entrance simultaneously, while another remained on the guard on the outside.

Mr. Harvey Kee, president of the bank, was at the teller's window, when one of the men stepped up and presenting a Winchester said, "Say, you d--- s--- of a b---, shell out your cash, and be d---d quick about it too." At the same time, noticing O. B. Kee, the cashier, at the books, he ordered his pal to attend to him.

The third bandit then went to a room in back of bank building where F. B. Hoyt lay very sick, and compelled him to get up to open the safe. Hoyt came in at the point of a Winchester and made an effort to open the safe but was so nervous that he did not succeed, although being roundly cursed for his delay and having a Winchester snapped in his face once or twice.

About this time, shooting commenced on the outside which so excited the bandits on the inside that they *grabbed up what money they could find on the top of the counter, (about $300) and skipped out. They could have got two thousand dollars by pulling out the tellers draw just below. As they were leaving, one of the fellows jerked off O. B. Kee's watch and put it into his pocket.*

On the opposite corner from the Lincoln County Bank, J. B. Mitchell has been conducting a barber shop. He was sitting out in front of his shop, and noticing the movements of the bandits called out "the Dalton gang in town," and got up and started to go into his shop, when the fellow in front of the bank, called to him to "shut up and sit down." He did not heed the admonition however, and started to go into his shop, when the bandit shot killing him instantly, the bullet entering on his right side, between the fourth and fifth ribs and piercing his body.

By this time there was a general fusillade between bandits and citizens, fully 100 shots being fired. As the robbers were mounting to ride off, N. W. Warren, a deputy U.S. marshal killed one of their horses, (since ascertained to be Bill Cook's) but the owner got up behind one of the others and all rode off in the same direction from whence they came – the Creek country.

Sheriff Parker immediately organized a posse and started in pursuit. At the edge of town another one of their horses was killed. They overtook an old German in a cart, took his horse out of the cart and rode on. They also made old man Pollard dismount and appropriated his horse also. The sheriff and posse came up on them near Chuck-a-hoe on section 36, 15-4, and a hundred or more shots were fired. One of the bandits were shot and taken prisoner. The others scattered through the woods and were lost track of. The sheriff and posse feeling that they had achieved enough glory for one day returned home. The prisoner captured is a young boy of the typical cowboy order, aged about 21 years. He gives his name as Elmer Lucas. He is shot through the hips the ball going through his body, making a painful and ugly, but not seriously fatal wound. He gives the names of the band of outlaws: Bill Cook, Tom Cook, Jack Starr or Cherokee Bill (a Cherokee Indian) and the prisoner. He says they are known as the Cook gang and that he joined them at the . . . . ranch in the Creek nation only last Monday.

J. B. Stewart, the liveryman says that he remembers that the horse that was killed, was put up at his stable last Friday. It is evident that they were posted, because they knew exactly how to get into the rear of the Lincoln county bank. One of the gang was seen in the rear of Hoffman, Charles & Conklin's bank about an hour before the hold-up. A number remember the fellows loafing around last night, (Sunday) and this morning one of them purchased two or three bottles of whiskey at Reeve's saloon.

Mr. Mitchell, the gentleman shot, was a quiet, unoffensive citizen aged fifty-three years. He leaves a wife and two daughters in straightened circumstances. The people are very much worked up over the affair and are in favor of meting out summary justice to all the gang should they be captured, but as they made directly for their haunts in the Creek country, and are now safely hiding in the canyons and caves of that section there is little hope of capturing them.

Cherokee Bill was one of the two outlaws out in front of the bank. When J. B. Mitchell started screaming about the bank, Mitchell tried to stand up from his chair, Cherokee Bill leveled his Winchester rifle and shot the barber at a distance of about 200 yards. Mitchell staggered a few feet and fell to the sidewalk near the corner of the barber shop. Mitchell died within minutes of being shot; he was fifty-three years old and left a wife and two young children.

When the outlaws came out of the bank they fired their guns wildly in all directions. W. N. Warren, a county deputy sheriff shot Bill Cook's horse, Cook mounted up behind one of his gang. The gang was closely pursued by a posse put together by Sheriff Claude Parker. There was a gunfight once Parker's posse chased the gang into some timber east of town. The *Edmond Sun Democrat* on August 3, 1894, said the gun battle lasted for fifteen minutes and over two hundred shots were exchanged.

One of the gang, Elmer Lucas, was wounded and captured by the posse. The rest of the gang was able to escape into the hills. Lucas was taken back to Chandler, but due to anger over the death of Mitchell and calls for a lynching, he was transported to the federal jail at Guthrie, capitol of the Oklahoma Territory. Lucas while in custody named the other members of the gang. According to him they were Cherokee Bill, Bill Cook, Henry Munson, Jack Starr, Tulsa Jack and Lon Gordon. Lucas also under interrogation confessed to his involvement in the train robbery at Red Rock. Later, he was transferred to the federal jail at Fort Smith, Arkansas, where he was indicted for the train robbery and recovered from his wounds.

On July 31, Deputy U. S. Marshal Scott Huffvine, an Indian resident of Kellyville, got information that the Cook Gang was going to meet on Polecat Creek in the Creek Nation. To be able to locate the gang, Huffvine got the most famous tracker in the Indian Territory to assist him. Tiger Jack was an Euchee Indian, a tribe that is closely aligned with the Creek Indians. Tiger Jack had worked with quite a few of the deputy U. S. marshals, especially Heck Thomas in tracking down desperadoes. Tiger Jack picked up the trail of the gang, but they were too late and the gang got away.

On August 9, Deputy U. S. Marshals Jesse Allen and Thompson Pickett, who were also Euchee Indians and members of the Creek Lighthorse Police with the aid of an Indian posse, located the Cook Gang. Allen and Pickett had been hunting the Cook Gang since the Red Fork robbery.

The gang had been hiding out fourteen miles west of Sapulpa, Creek Nation, in the home of Bill Province, the uncle of Henry Munson. It was early in the morning and the gang was outside the home washing up, the posse, about a dozen strong, came in with guns blazing at 8 a.m. A desperate gun battle ensued which resulted in about forty shots being fired between the parties. Henry Munson was killed and Lon Gordon was severely wounded, Curtis Dayson was captured, one Indian policeman was wounded. Cherokee Bill, Bill Cook, Thurman Baldwin and Buck Snyder were able to escape a close call. Gordon later died from his injuries, gunshots to the head and lungs, after being taken to Sapulpa.

For women, Cherokee Bill was said to have irresistible charm. He was said to have a sweetheart in nearly every section of the territory. Cherokee Bill was often protected from harm by loyal friends and a violent reputation. Lawmen that pursued him, hearing of his deadly rifle accuracy and fast six-shooter action, kept a safe distance and many times avoided engaging him in battle. Because he was on good terms with Cherokees, Creeks and Seminoles, he moved easily through their villages and lands, something his pursuers could not do.

From the time Cherokee Bill joined the Cook brothers, he acted as though he was destined to die in two years and wanted to kill as many men as he could. Some of the fugitives who allied themselves to the Cook Gang that summer of 1894 were killed in desperate fights with deputy U. S. marshals; others were captured and given penitentiary sentences.

Chapter Six

Robbers' Roost

The Indian Territory was quiet for awhile, the deputy U.S. marshals were hunting for Cherokee Bill and the Cook Gang but no solid information or leads were coming forward. It was as if the gang had just disappeared.

On the late summer night of September 14, 1894, in the Creek Nation capital of Okmulgee, around 10 p.m., some strangers rode into town. Cherokee Bill, Thurman Baldwin, Jess Snyder and Bill Cook went directly and tied up in front of the largest store in Okmulgee and one of the largest stores in the Indian Territory, J. A. Parkinson & Company. Even at the late hour, the store was still open. They entered with guns drawn and immediately demanded for what cash was in the store. The store employees handed over $600 in cash. They left the store and mounted up and left as cool and calm as they came in. The town was quiet during the robbery because most of the citizens were attending a Creek Indian stick ball game a few miles south of town.

On the night of October 4, after 10 p.m., six masked and heavily armed men rode up to the Arkansas Valley Railroad station platform at Wagoner, Creek Nation, and dismounted. There were a few people in the depot waiting for the southbound passenger train from Kansas City, which was a quarter hour late. Three outlaws with drawn pistols stood guard, while the other three went in the depot and made the station agent open the safe and hand over $300 in cash.

Upon leaving the depot, the gang fired forty to fifty gunshots, completely terrifying the town.

The same six bandits got a ferry ride across the Arkansas River between Fort Gibson and Muskogee on October 5. Not leaving the area immediately, they held up and robbed Ed Ayers, a Cherokee of $120 on the Muskogee-Fort Gibson road. The gang was identified as Cherokee Bill, Jim French, Bill Cook, Jess Snyder, Sam McWilliams, *alias* "The Verdigris Kid" and Thurman Baldwin.

The desperadoes went back across the Arkansas River and camped between the Verdigris and Grand Rivers below Gibson Station near the Katy Railroad tracks. On the morning of October 9, they headed north. Near Wagoner, they separated; Cook and two members of the gang were riding northwest along the Arkansas Valley track, which was owned by the Missouri Pacific Railroad, towards Claremore, Cherokee Nation. Cherokee Bill and the other two members headed north along the M. K. & T. Railroad tracks toward Chouteau, Cherokee Nation.

On arriving at Bull Creek on the Valley line, the Cook faction robbed the entire work crew of coal miners, getting about $200, then rode on towards Claremore, which they reached at 9 p.m. They intended to rob the depot at Inola but there was a large group of cowboys who had recently came in from a roundup, so they rode on to Claremore.

A local freight train crew had seen some suspicious riders and alerted the Claremore station agent, who proceeded to put all his money on a passenger train which arrived only minutes before Cook and his crew got there. The station agent slipped out the back door and notified the authorities. Deputy Police Chief Pink Chambers was the first to arrive at the depot. When he got near the depot, the outlaws got the upper hand on him and made him dismount and proceeded to rob him of his pistols, gold watch, and several dollars. Cook and crew marched him along with them until they reached their horses; they mounted up and rode off into the darkness. A posse from Claremore tried to pursue but came up empty as they lost the trail.

Cherokee Bill was much more successful with his merry band of outlaws. They first struck at Chouteau in the Cherokee Nation. They arrived after nightfall on October 9, and when straight to the M. K. & T. Railroad depot. They took $35 dollars from the night manager, Mr. Fultz. Then they robbed the American Express Co. agent, James A. Quinn, of silver dollars, half dollars, quarters, dimes, and gold and silver certificates, all carried away in a sack. After telling everyone to stay cool and calm they rode off into the night.

On Saturday, October 20, 1894 a Missouri Pacific express train was held up five miles south of Wagoner at Corretta siding. Most people at the time felt this was the work of Cherokee Bill and Bill Cook. The *Daily Oklahoman* newspaper reported on October 23, 1894:

> *The train was going at a speed of about twenty-five miles per hour and when within 100 feet of the switch, a man sprang from behind an embankment and threw the switch for the side track, running the train into a string of empty box cars. Engineer James Harris applied the air and reversed his engine, but did not have time to jump before the engine struck the cars on the siding. Two of the robbers ran to the engine and commanded Engineer Harris and Fireman Cottrell to come down, and as soon as they had dismounted, marched them to the baggage and express cars, where, by firing through the doors, they forced Messenger Ford to admit them. Meanwhile, two more of*

the robbers had taken up positions at the rear of the train to prevent anyone escaping through the rear doors of the sleeper, two more mounted the platform between the smoker and the baggage car and two more, the platform between the first and second coaches; all keeping up a continual firing. During this time, the two in the express car were ransacking it. They got all the money in the local safe and Messenger Ford's gun, and then commanded him to open the through safe. He told them it was impossible, and after hearing his explanation as to how it was locked, they left the express car.

The two robbers on the front platform started through the second coach demanding money and valuables. As soon as they reached the rear of the coach, the two men on the platform started through the second coach. When they were about half way through this car, a freight train followed close behind whistled and Bill Cook, the leader who had all the time remained outside issuing commands, swearing at the passengers and shooting, called for all hands to come out. The men on the cars jumped out, and when all were outside fired a last volley at the train and disappeared in the darkness.

Jack Mahara, an advance agent for Mahara's Minstrel Company, was struck in the forehead by a bullet and seriously injured. Walter Barnes of Van Buren, Arkansas, was slightly injured by a piece of bullet striking him in the cheek . . . Special officers Helmick and Dickson of the Missouri Pacific were on the train, also Deputy Marshals Heck Bruner and Joe Casaver, but the attack was so sudden that they were all covered by Winchesters in the hands of the bandits before they had time to make a move. Casaver lost a watch and his six-shooter in the fracas . . . The train was backed to Wagoner for assistance and to give medical attention to the injured. The entire train was completely riddled with bullets, every window being broken and the engine cab shot to pieces, even the steam gauge and gauge pump, being shot away.

The newspapers reported that there were eight or ten men in the gang with two of them being white. The rest were reported to black men or half-breeds who didn't attempt to hide their faces. They even noted that it could have been white men with blackened faces.

This robbery was not done by the Cook Gang, it was a majority black gang led by the notorious black Creek outlaw, Buss Luckey, who sometimes had rode with the Cook Gang. Many months later the *Vinita Indian Chieftain* on June 18, 1896, gave the following information on the train robbery:

The participants in the Corretta Train robbery . . . were made public for the first time during the trial of Bob Elzey. Henry and Frank Smith, who pleaded guilty to the charge, went on the stand and testified that Buz Luckey organized the band and that it was composed of Lucky, Will White, Elzey, Frank, Henry and Will Smith.

Later Cherokee Bill talked about this robbery after his incarceration. The *Muskogee Phoenix* newspaper on October 8, 1896, carried the story:

. . . Jailer Berry, George Lawson, the hangman, and several other attaches were taking a sun bath on the veranda of the Federal jail at Fort Smith the other morning, all in a reminiscent mood, when someone mentioned the name of Cherokee Bill.

I was amused at Cherokee Bill the last time we had him

out to attend court," spoke the affable jailer. It was when we took him over to be arraigned with the Smith boys for the Corretta train robbery. I had never said anything to Bill about that job so on the way back from the courthouse I asked if he was in the hold-up.

'No,' he said, 'I was lost down in the bottom that night and didn't know where I was until I heard the train whistle. Then I wished I was nearer the track, so I could hold the blamed thing up.'

Cherokee Bill, Bill Cook, Skeeter, Jim French and Verdigris Kid had come down from the hills up on the Grand River that day," added George Lawson who trailed the Cook gang all over the territory during their memorable reign of terror and had the satisfaction of finally bringing in Cherokee Bill.

They crossed under the bridge on Grand River and struck off into the bottom but it was a terrible bad night, dark and rainy, and as they were following the trails instead of the roads, they all got tangled up some way down there and hardly knew which way they were going. When the train whistled it gave them an idea of the location of the railroad track and from that they were able to make their way out.

The whole gang said they wished they had been nearer the track, and if they had been they would have robbed the train for they were all dead broke. They were too far away, though, to reach the track before the train had passed, so they went on toward Muskogee. They had gone hardly a mile before they heard a lot of shooting and they knew just exactly what had happened. Another crowd had held up the train and was robbing it.

During the train robbery at Corretta siding about two hundred gun shots were fired by the gang and they got away with $500 plus valuables from the passengers. By this time, panic reigned in the northern half of the Indian Territory and names of Cherokee Bill and the Cook Gang was on everyone's lips. Union Agency Indian Agent Dew M. Wisdom sent a wire to the Office of Indian Affairs in Washington, D.C., which stated:

> *My police force is not equal to the emergency, and Marshal Crump at Fort Smith writes that he has not the money to keep marshals in the field for a campaign. Affairs here are in a desperate condition; business is suspended, the people generally intimidated and private individuals robbed every day and night. I renew my recommendations and earnestly insist that the government, through the proper channel, take the manner in hand to protect its court and citizens of the United States, who are lawful residents of the territory. Licensed traders are especially suffering, and they are here under suspense. The state of siege must be broken and something gone to save life and property.*

Marshal Crump of the Fort Smith federal court was summoned to Washington, D. C., to give a full account of the operation of the Cook Gang and Cherokee Bill. The U. S. Attorney General pledged the government's full cooperation. The Secretary of War threatened "to abrogate the treaties, abolish tribal relations and establish a territorial government." The U. S. Attorney General authorized the posting of the rewards for the capture of any or all of the Cook Gang, as did Principal Chief J. C. Harris of the Cherokee Nation.

Clarence O. Warren, a white settler in the Creek Nation, gave an account in the *Indian Pioneer Papers* of how Cherokee Bill and the Cook Gang got their ammunition for their guns:

> . . . And something else about the Cook Bros. and Cherokee Bill. They of necessity had to have ammunition, a lot of it, guns and shells, sometimes they had money and sometimes they didn't, but they had a way of getting the ammunition which worked it they were out of funds. As I said, my uncle Jim Kgan, had a store at Sapulpa. The manager of this store was another uncle of mine, Bert Gray. He said it was he who sold ammunition to these outlaws. They would come in usually when my uncle was alone and tell him what they wanted and how much. So, of course, they got it, and on short order, for he was anxious to get rid of them as soon as possible. But they always asked how much the bill was, and for my uncle to keep account of it for they would return later and pay it; and the unusual thing about it, they always slipped in when they had money and paid their bill.
>
> Well, later, I think it was after the capture of Cherokee Bill, and during his trial at Fort Smith, that the question of where and how they got their guns and ammunition came up. This led to an investigation and it was found that they bought it at Sapulpa, and at the Kgan store. So Bert Gray, being manager of the store was summoned to appear at Fort Smith, by Judge Parker, the Federal Judge of that district, as a witness, and to tell just what he knew about the matter. Well, he related to the court the story as told here and wound up by saying, "Judge when fellows like that come in and put their six shooters on you, that makes their credit mighty good with me." This created a lot of laughing and seemed to be a good explanation as to how and why

the Kgan store sold them ammunition. It seemed anybody, especially the Cook Brothers and Cherokee Bill, could open an account with six shooters.

Ashley Guffey another early resident of the Indian Territory told of another incident with Cherokee Bill in the *Indian Pioneer Papers*:

> *. . . While we lived here, Cherokee Bill made us a visit, came one night and wanted to spend the night with us. Of course, we didn't refuse him. He was very courteous, and seemed to appreciate our hospitality. His reason for coming to our place, he explained, was that he was being chased by the U.S. Marshals, who had run him out of the Osage country, where, he said, he had been selling whiskey.*

In the meantime, Jim Cook was being held in the Cherokee National Prison in Tahlequah for the killing of Sequoyah Houston. His trial was set for October 29, 1894. The prison was heavily guarded due to word of the Cook Gang trying to free Jim. The attack from the gang never came, but Jim tried to escape from the prison guards on Sunday, October 21, when they allowed him to go hunting with them while he was manacled at ankle and waist. The guards quickly got Jim as he tried to run away. His case was reset in the Cherokee courts for November 13, where he was sentenced to eight years in the Cherokee National Prison.

Cherokee Bill spent most of his time hiding out in the northern Cherokee Nation east of the present town of Nowata, Oklahoma, near the Verdigris River. This area was heavily populated with Cherokee Freedmen. Many of the best cowboys of the Indian Territory cattle ranches were black men who were descendants of Cherokee and Creek Freedmen. Will Rogers was from Claremore, Cherokee Nation, and he learned to ride and rope from the top cowhand on his father's ranch, a Cherokee Freedman named Daniel Walker, who was from Fort Gibson. Walker also served as a posse man for deputy U. S. marshals from time to time. Claremore is the same town that the popular musical *Oklahoma* is based in.

By late October, Cherokee Bill and Bill Cook had parted company for good and Cherokee Bill was leading his own raids at this time in his criminal career. It appears that two of the white members of the gang, Skeeter Baldwin and Jess Snyder stayed with Bill Cook and the other gang members followed Cherokee Bill.

At 7 p.m., Monday night, October 22, 1894, Cherokee Bill and three desperados looted the small town of Watova located on the Missouri Pacific Railroad line, six miles south of Nowata. The gang robbed two stores and the post office of $400. The locals said that Cherokee Bill took the first store keeper as a hostage to the second store, and then took the two store keepers to the post office. It was also during this period that Cherokee Bill and gang robbed the town of Talala, Cherokee Nation. It was said that Bill and gang rode into the small town and noticed it was nearly deserted. Most of the inhabitants were attending a baseball game nearby. Cherokee Bill started on one end of the main street and robbed every business on the street, and then he and his gang rode out of town.

A grand jury at the Fort Smith federal jail indicted Curtis Dayson and Elmer Lucas for the Red Fork train robbery on October 24, 1894. Curtis Dayson was found guilty and Elmer Lucas was found guilty of complicity in the robbery since he only held the horses. Both men were sent to the Detroit House of Corrections. Judge Isaac C. Parker gave Dayson fifteen years and Lucas received ten years of imprisonment on November 10.

The Union Agency Indian Agent Wisdom telegraphed U.S. Marshal Crump at Fort Smith on October 31. He informed the federal authorities that he had reliable information that the Cook Gang was camping on Blue Creek, twelve miles north of Muskogee. The Indian agent felt that the gang was going to make a move on the Muskogee bank. Crump telegraphed six of his deputies who were stationed in the Cherokee Nation to report to Muskogee at once. But there was no sign of the gang anywhere near Muskogee.

Cherokee Bill next struck at the small cattle town of Lenapah, Cherokee Nation, which was also on the Missouri Pacific's Kansas and Arkansas Valley line and had about 200 inhabitants. The town's principal business was the H. C. Schufeldt & Son Store, which supplied much of the northern Cooweescoowee District of the Cherokee Nation and handled a great deal of money. Lenapah is fifteen miles south of Coffeyville, Kansas, where the Dalton Gang was wiped out in 1892.

Just before noon on November 9, 1894, Cherokee Bill and the "Verdigris Kid" McWilliams rode rapidly into Lenapah from the south. They attracted very little attention because their appearance differed little from the hundreds of cowboys who came into town to trade. As soon as they dismounted in front of the Schufeldt store, they mounted the platform of the cotton wagon weighing scales, Winchesters drawn. McWilliams guarded the outside of the building and Cherokee Bill went inside the store. The first thing Bill said was "Hands up!," which John Shufeldt and two customers did immediately. The customers were lined up against the wall and the store owner was told to open the safe and sack up the contents. Schufeldt put gold and silver coins, gold and silver certificates and bank notes in the bag totaling $600. Cherokee Bill also robbed the customers and Schufeldt, getting from the latter a gold watch locket, for about another $100.

Outside, McWilliams was firing warning shots at citizens coming toward the store. Needing ammunition, Cherokee Bill asked where it was located, and Schufeldt told him in the back room of the store. There was a narrow vacant lot between and a parallel restaurant next door, the interior of which was being wallpapered. A man by the name of Ernest Melton from Paris, Texas, was doing the work along with several others. When they heard the shots fired by McWilliams, they all rushed to the window to see what was happening.

Cherokee Bill flicked a glance at the window and saw Melton staring at him. For the hell of it, Cherokee Bill threw his rifle to his shoulder and fired a shot at Melton that pierced his brain and killed him. After this incident the federal court at Fort Smith, Arkansas, put up a $1,300 bounty, "Dead or Alive," on Cherokee Bill. He became the most feared outlaw in the annals of the Indian Territory. To help the reader gauge the fear of Cherokee Bill we will note an item from the *Eufaula Indian Journal* dated February 1, 1895:

> *The citizens of Lenapah, I.T., have evidently been thoroughly cowed by the outlaw Cherokee Bill. At the last meeting of the village council they passed an ordinance which grants to that worthy the privilege of coming and going there whenever he desires, and they guarantee him protection from molestation.*

In all my research, I have never seen a town or village

pass an ordinance to protect an outlaw if they were within the limits of the municipality. This is fear taken to another level of comprehension.

Deputy U.S. Marshals Bill Smith and George Lawson working out of Sapulpa, where trying their best to locate Cherokee Bill. They learned that Cherokee Bill and his gang had been seen at a trail crossing near the Arkansas River, near the home of Charles Patton.

Patton had gotten friendly with McWilliams in earlier days by working livestock on the Verdigris River. The deputy marshals promised they would split any reward if Patton could locate the outlaws. He had seen the outlaws near his home and told the outlaws he would locate them.

Patton located the desperados and stayed with them for about six hours. Cherokee Bill told Patton he had shot someone in Lenapah during a robbery. McWilliams gave Patton the gold watch locket that Cherokee Bill had taken from Shufeldt. Later that night Patton met Smith and Lawson in Sapulpa and told them all he learned and gave them the locket. Patton told the lawmen that Cherokee Bill mentioned he was trying to see a girlfriend named Maggie Glass and he would be staying at the home of Frank Daniels. Daniels was a Cherokee Freedman who lived earlier on Fourteen Mile Creek and was now living on the Caney River, ten miles west of Talala, Cherokee Nation.

Chapter Seven

The Manhunt

Sixteen men in a federal posse led by legendary lawmen Heck Thomas and Heck Bruner departed Fort Smith headed for the Caney. They arrived at the Frank Daniels' homestead in the Cherokee Nation late Friday afternoon, November 16, 1894. The lawmen found Daniels, his wife, and half brother home but no outlaws. The posse told the family to take shelter in the storm cellar. They concealed their horses in the woods and set up an ambush for Cherokee Bill and his gang, for they expected them to show up soon.

Burl Taylor, Daniel's half brother, interviewed for the *Indian Pioneer Papers* told what happened next:

I saw a battle between a posse and Cherokee Bill, Sam McWilliams and Texas Jack. This happened at my half brother's house, whose name was Frank Daniels. He lived on Caney River about five miles from Ramona. Deputy U.S. Marshal Heck Thomas, out of Fort Smith with sixteen deputized in his posse, came to Frank's home and told him that Cherokee Bill, Sam and Texas Jack were coming there, (don't know how they knew of their coming) and that Frank, his wife and I had better go somewhere as there was going to be plenty shooting and we might get hit. Frank told him that we could just go to the cellar, there were several out-buildings also built of logs. They hid the horses and stationed themselves in the house and out-buildings.

It was not long until Cherokee and his friends showed up; they rode to the horse-lot, just as they got to the gate one of the posse outside got excited and fired at them, just hit the edge of Cherokee's leg, killing his horse. When the posseman fired this shot, they all began firing at the outlaws; Texas Jack's horse was hit but not killed.

Texas Jack made a break for the timber and never did show up anymore. When Cherokee's horse was shot from under him, he got his Winchester and stood there in the wide-open pumping shots from his Winchester. Sam McWilliams horse was shot down and Sam was shot through the leg but not bad. He lost his Winchester when his horse was shot down, he crawled around in the high grass until he found it, then came to Cherokee's side, raised up and began firing – helping Cherokee out. Cherokee told Sam that he just had one more shot left in his gun and that there was a damn Law kept sticking his foot around the corner of the smoke-house and he was going to get it the next time he stuck it out, and then they would make a run for it. Sure enough, the fellow stuck his boot out again and Cherokee made a good hit. The fellow let out a cry and started hobbling toward the house, when he did this; Sam shot at him three times, knocking him down with the last shot but did not kill him. Cherokee and Sam then made a run for the timber, the way the bullets were hitting the dust around them as they crossed the road, we were looking for them to be shot down any minute, but they made it safely, the posse was afraid to go in the woods after them.

After the posse left, Cherokee and Sam came back to the house and got their saddles and bridles, borrowed two horses from Frank, went about two miles and roped two horses from a pasture belonging to a neighbor of Frank's and brought his horse back. We asked what became of Texas Jack, they told us that they had a pretty good bunch of money and it was in Jack's saddle bags, and they told him to beat it with the money.

In the *Fort Smith News-Record* on November 21, 1894, Heck Thomas was interviewed by a reporter concerning the shoot-out. Thomas said, "Just to think, after I had worked for weeks and spent upwards of $200 of my own money, to lose it all because they could not wait. I told them not to fire, but they did, and spoiled the game."

Thomas would not make another attempt to capture or kill the dangerous Cherokee Bill. Many years later the *Daily Oklahoman* newspaper of Oklahoma City ran an article on veteran lawmen of the Oklahoma/Indian Territories titled "Little Stories of Men Whose Lives Overflow with Danger; Wildest Tales of Adventure and Excitement Never Equalled the Real Histories of United States Marshal and Deputies Now Working in State of Oklahoma," on January 8, 1911. A group of lawmen including Thomas were reminiscing about the old days.

Legendary lawman Heck Thomas (front left).

One of the deputy U.S. marshals, John Paul Jones called Cherokee Bill a "human hyena" and Heck Thomas referred to him as "that nigger-Indian mixture of all that was bad."

According to the *Fort Smith Elevator* of March 20, 1896, Deputy U.S. Marshal Heck Bruner was the posse man who fired the first shot in the gunfight at the Daniel's homestead. Cherokee Bill is quoted as saying, "If I could see to pick out Heck Bruner, I'd like to get him."

Bruner was a noted Indian Territory marshal of Cherokee heritage who lived at Vinita, Cherokee Nation. He was involved in quite a few captures and killings of outlaws in the territory, including Ned Christie. Bruner and Bill would later have a date of destiny at Fort Smith during an aborted jail break attempt.

A prominent member of the Cherokee Council from Claremore on his way home met Cherokee Bill and McWilliams on the trail between Wagoner and Inola. He said that Cherokee Bill was in a talkative mood and jokingly said, "that the marshals nearly shot his winter clothes off."

The council member said that the bandits were heavily armed, looked tired and he was fearful they would ask for a horse trade, for their horses looked spent. Cherokee Bill told him that he would die with his boots on and he would also make sure some of the marshals would bite the dust also, when he did. Cherokee Bill was a tough hombre.

In December of 1894, Cherokee Bill and Jim French and an unknown accomplice held up the Missouri Pacific depot at Nowata. A few weeks later he held up the same station again. The *Eufaula Indian Journal* newspaper described what happened:

The Nowata Hold-Up

Claremore, I.T., Jan.1. – About 8:30 o'clock last night, just five minutes before the north bound passenger on the Kansas and Arkansas Valley road reached Nowata, Cherokee Bill, alone and unaided, robbed the station at that place.

He first ordered the hotel porter to put his lantern on his head and back into the station and followed him in. Station agent Bristow saw the situation and at once handed out the money in the safe, between $14 and $15.

Bill then ordered Bristow to walk ahead of him, leaving the porter in the office. Only three persons were in the waiting-room, and they were ordered to keep quiet. Station Agent Bristow had sent in his resignation and balanced up his books, and his last official act was to turn over the cash to Cherokee Bill, Bristow's successor arriving on the passenger train about five minutes later.

This is the second hold-up here in two weeks, Jim French and Cherokee Bill leading the other band.

Cherokee Bill seemed anxious to crowd all the crime he could into the old year, having killed his brother-in-law, Brown, night before last. It seems that Brown abused his wife, Cherokee Bill's sister, and Cherokee went to the Brown place and ordered Brown to leave. Brown didn't go fast enough, and Cherokee Bill pumped a stream of fire into him, shooting him seven times with a Winchester. Cherokee Bill was in Nowata yesterday afternoon, and is believed to be on the Verdigris, east of Nowata at the present.

On Sunday afternoon, on the prairie about five miles east of Talala, six horsemen wee training their horses to carry double and to allow the riders to mount rapidly. Cherokee Bill was recognized as one of them. It is believed that he is organizing a band of his own. The trainmen are daily in fear of being held up.

The popular story on Cherokee Bill as printed in *Hell on the Border* was that he shot his brother-in-law over some hogs. This story was not true but repeated on many occasions for various western history writers. Cherokee Bill's sister, Georgia Goldsby, had married an older man named Mose Brown, who couldn't get along with Cherokee at all. Georgia's daughter, Maud, in an interview that was recorded in the *Indian Pioneer Papers*:

> . . . Shortly after this trouble, and Crawford had returned to the home place where he was staying, he wrote to my mother asking her to come and see him, which was only natural as she was his only sister and closest advisor. Father learned of her intended trip to see Crawford and objected to her going, and when he saw he could not prevent her from going he told her he was going with her. Mother tried to persuade him not to go and told him, "You know that you always mistreated Crawford and was the cause of him leaving home once, and he told you that he would kill you some day if you didn't leave him alone, and you had best not go about him or molest him again.
>
> However, when Mother went aboard the train at Fort Gibson, Father also boarded the same train at another place without Mother knowing of his presence on the train. When she got off the train at Nowata where she was to take livery conveyance out to the place, to her surprise there stood Father on the station platform. Mother again tried to persuade him not to go out to the farm with Mother. Upon their arrival at Crawford's place, Crawford asked him why he came, and during the altercation that followed, Crawford shot and killed my father. That sad occurrence happened in September [November], 1894, when I was only

nine-months-old. Shortly after the death of my father, I was taken into the home and care of my grandmother, Ellen Lynch, at Fort Gibson where I was reared.

It is understandable that Maud would have the months wrong; she was only nine-months-old when the event happened and she was interviewed in 1938, many years later. I believe this story is closer to the truth than other stories on what occurred between Bill and Mose Brown.

Chapter Eight

Isaac "Ike" Rogers

Ike Rogers was born either in 1844 or 1850 as a slave in the Cherokee Nation. He was rumored to be a relative of Clement Vann Rogers, father of Will Rogers. Ike's mother was Martha Richardson *aka* Martha May. He was a slave of mixed-blood Cherokees Elzira May and her husband Peter May. His father, name unknown, was most likely a mixed-blood Cherokee. A mixed-blood Indian is one with European ancestry. An Indian with African blood was called a half-breed in the Indian Territory. Most of the slave owners in the Cherokee Nation were mixed-blood Indians.

The well known Agnes Walker, housekeeper for Clem Van Rogers, father of Will, and wife of the famous black cowboy Daniel Walker, said she was a first cousin of Ike Rogers. Looking at all that went on during slavery, Ike very well may be related to Will Rogers as well. Daniel Walker taught Will Rogers to ride and rope, and was the foreman on Clem Van Roger's ranch. Walker was also a member of federal posses from time to time in the Cherokee Nation when manhunts were necessary; one of the lawmen he worked with was Bud Ledbetter.

Ike grew up in the Indian Territory during the antebellum years. He enlisted in the Union army after the outbreak of the Civil War. Ike enlisted in one of the first African American units organized. The First Kansas Colored Volunteer Infantry Regiment that was the inspiration of Kansas

Senator James Henry Lane. Ike's muster card states he was in Company E, age of eighteen, and he stood five feet, five inches, enrollment was at Mound City, Kansas.

If this age is correct, Ike was born in 1844, the 1850 birth date would have him enlisting at the age of twelve, which is possible if he was big for his age but not probable. The information on the muster card shows that Ike was there at the very beginning of this storied regiment. This black regiment was seen as a Kansas militia unit since the United States had not officially recognized black troops in the fall of 1862.

The first action the 1st Kansas Infantry saw was at the Battle of Island Mound in Bates County, Missouri, on October 29, 1862. The battle was the first engagement by a black Union regiment in the Civil War. It is a very good possibility that Ike was in this battle. The first black soldiers to see action in the Civil War were those in the 1st Native Home Guard Regiment from the Indian Territory.

Most of the non-commissioned officers in this unit were black Indian Freedmen who served as interpreters for the white officers. The 1st Native Home Guard Regiment was primarily Creek and Seminole Indians

Deputy U.S. Marshal Ike Rogers

along with black members of those tribes. In the 1st Kansas Infantry that Ike served in, most of the men in Company E were Indian Freedmen recruits from the Indian Territory.

The most famous battle of the Civil War that the 1st Kansas Infantry served in was the Battle of Honey Springs in July of 1863 in the Indian Territory. The regiment defended Fort Smith, Arkansas, from Confederate attack in 1864. One of the official reports said the 1st Kansas entered the battlefield like they were on dress parade. Ike was mustered out at Pine Bluff, Arkansas, on October 1, 1865. Following the war, Rogers took his family from Fort Scott, Kansas, back to the Cherokee Nation, where according to a descendant, Nicka Smith, Rogers said, "My cousin told me not to come here to live, I told him, 'You have schools here, and my children have Cherokee blood in their veins and have a right to attend them.' "

After the war, Ike went back home to the Cherokee Nation. He built a small farm and was married four times, two of whom were sisters, and had eight children. Ike served sometimes as a posseman for deputy U.S. marshals working out of the Fort Smith federal court. Jim Vaughn, a resident of the Indian Territory that lived at Paden, said:

> . . . *Ike Rogers was a Negro United States Marshal in the territorial days during the days of Cherokee Bill. He was often in the company of Bass Reeves, another Negro United States Marshal, when covering trails leading out from Keokuk Falls and over into the eastern part of the Territory.*

In May of 1885, Ike was one of several Cherokee Freedmen who gave testimony on the treatment of black citizens of the Cherokee Nation. This Q & A session was with a U.S. Senate Subcommittee from Washington D.C., at Muskogee,

Indian Territory. This was an initiative by the Committee on Indian Affairs of the United States Senate. Some of the interview with Ike Rogers follows:

Q: You are a freedman now?

A: Yes

Q: Will you tell us how the freedmen have been treated by the Cherokee? We want to all the information you can give us upon that subject.

A: We have been recognized under that treaty as citizens only in part, but never in full according to the terms of the treaty; that is, we have been allowed to live in the country, and we have been allowed to vote, &c.; but in such things as enjoying the full privileges of the schools we have, we have not been treated as the other people in the nation. There are a great many colored people who came here before the treaty was made, and who were here at the making of the treaty, can produce evidence that they came in the limit of time, have been worked against through the census-takers, and have been treated as intruders. . .

Q: Are you allowed to live peaceably?

A: There have been many cases in which we have been assaulted.

Q: Were not the parties punished?

A: No sir; our people have been assaulted and killed, and nothing has been done to the parties who did it.

Q: Has nobody been prosecuted under the Law?

A: No, Sir.

Chairman –
Q: Do your people bring suits in the courts here?

A: Yes, Sir.

Q: Do they try one of your people different from a Cherokee?

A: They do whatever they please with him if a Cherokee is against a colored person they bring in any kind of evidence.

Mr. Ingalls –

Q: If a Cherokee shoots you on your farm, would the Cherokee be tried under the laws of the nation?

A: One citizen can shoot another, and if the other gets well that settles the matter.

Q: Have you no laws for the punishment of crime?

A: No Sir; we have had none heretofore. The man probably gets out until the other one gets well . . .

Q: Do you know how a white man or Negro is treated who comes from outside and marries a Cherokee woman? Do they have the same recognition?

A: I can say that a white man when he comes here and marries a Cherokee woman by blood, has the right to vote, and enjoys all the rights which are guaranteed to him by the law; but when a colored man comes here, with the same certificate the white man has, he does not fare the same.

Mr. Ingalls –

Q: You refer to a colored man who comes from outside?

A: Yes, Sir.

Q: Do you know how many of these freedmen were made free the Treaty of 1866?

A: No Sir; I do not. But I think it was somewhere near 19,000. There is a census of them, though.

This interview with the U.S. Senate Subcommittee probably didn't endear Ike Rogers with the Cherokee political leadership. The subcommittee was interested in the status of Indian Freedmen, the conditions in the Indian Territory, and how the Five Civilized Nations were doing. I am sure they would use the information for the *Curtis Act*, the legislative trigger of the Dawes Commission which saw the end of the sovereign Indian Nations. Ike Rogers had served in the U.S. military, worked with federal lawmen, and I am sure his word had some gravity with the Freedmen interviews. What type of retribution would Ike suffer because of this, we can only conjecture but we will never know for sure. The whole matter seems to be a 19th century version of *Black Lives Matter*.

When Ike first became a commissioned deputy U.S. marshal is not known. The National Archives records, which are not complete, show Ike did receive commissions from the Fort Smith federal court as a deputy U.S. marshal on October 4, 1892, June 1, 1893, and January 10, 1895. The last commission came right before the capture of Cherokee Bill. During the 1890s, Henry Starr was a noted Cherokee Indian bank robber and had killed a deputy U.S. marshal in the Cherokee Nation. In his autobiography Starr talked about Ike Rogers and Rufus Cannon, black federal lawmen dogging his trail during a manhunt:

. . . I had met my mother and sister by appointment at the home of J. O. Morrison, on the prairie nine miles northwest of Nowata, and I heard afterwards my treacherous stepfather had told the deputies to get me. As they approached the house, I was undetermined what to do. At that time I was paying attention to Mr. Morrison's daughter, May,

and in her presence I would not run. Perish forever the thought: There were several ladies present, and they pleaded with me not to kill the officers. "Ladies," I replied, "It is not a question of my killing them but of keeping them from killing me!" I kept out of sight in the hall at the head of the stairs with my rifle drawn, and could have killed them as easy as shooting two rabbits had I so desired. Both knew I was in the house, for they had discovered my well known horse tied in the barn, but at the time each assured the other that I was not any place around. As they started off, I watched them from the window, Roger's hat blew off as he passed the window, and he looked up, but I had covered and he only pulled his hat over his eyes and went on without looking back. They made no attempt at my arrest, and I could tell by their actions that they did not want me very bad.

Henry Starr had another run in with Deputy U.S. Marshals Ike Rogers and Rufus Cannon on the evening of January 20, 1893. This time Rogers and Cannon had an Indian police posse of fifteen men with them. Near Bartlesville, they had a running gunfight with Starr's gang, which included two white men, Ed Newcome and Jesse Jackson. In the gunfight, Cannon shot off Jackson's right arm and sent another bullet through his side with a shotgun before he was captured.

Starr and Newcome managed to escape. Ike Rogers sent a telegram to U.S. Marshal Yoes at Fort Smith, stating that "about 200 shots were fired," the captured outlaw would "possibly recover," and "we are now on the trail of Starr and his confederate and will yet run them down. We are determined to rid society of this gang."

Henry Starr

Jackson was picked up at Bartlesville, Cherokee Nation, by Deputy U.S. Marshal Heck Thomas on charges of robbing a Santa Fe Railway passenger train on November 8, 1892, at Wharton (now Perry), Oklahoma Territory. But we can see by this information that Ike Rogers was in charge of this federal posse and manhunt and sent a concise note to the U.S. marshal at Fort Smith in regards to the engagement.

In regards to the second robbery by Cherokee Bill at Nowata, many years later the station agent, George Bristow, was interviewed at the age of 100 by Olivia E. Myers a writer for the *Frontier Times* magazine on October 10, 1966. In the interview he stated:

> . . . *When Ike Rogers, a half-Negro, half-Indian freedman who lived about five miles east of Nowata down on the Verdigris River near the Coodys' Bluff ford, came in and bought a money order to order whiskey – and paid for it with a $20 bill that had a small round hole right through*

the center – I knew that $20 bill. It was one I had placed in an envelope the night I was robbed.

This made me suspect that Cherokee was holing up at Ike Rogers', for the whole country knew that Cherokee Bill was sweet on a half-white, half-Cherokee girl named Maggie Glass. She often met Cherokee at the Rogers' home for she had been forbidden to see him at her parents.

By the way, this is departing from my story, but another fellow who thought of himself a toughy (sic) was stuck on Maggie, and he had talked around that he would Kill Cherokee Bill if he ever got him in pistol range. This fellow came face to face with Cherokee Bill just as he came up out of the old ford at Coody's Bluff. Cherokee Bill told him that he'd been told he was going to kill him. He made the man get down off his horse, throw away his .45 and then told him to get down on his stomach like the dog he was and eat grass. The man ate grass. Bill then told him if he ever heard of him even carrying a gun, he'd come back and kill him. The man was never known to carry a gun again as long as Cherokee Bill was loose. Cherokee was bad business. Real bad business.

. . . When I saw that $20 bill with the hole in it, I never let on but I made a point of showing Ike how I'd fixed a little block of wood to wedge in the safe so the lock would not snap each time I opened it during the working hours. I told him at close of business, I removed the block so the safe would lock while I was away.

When Cherokee Bill came to rob me the second time, I knew for sure he was in cahoots with Rogers when he never ordered me to open the safe. He just said, "Hand it over."

As soon as news of the holdup got around, Clint Scales and the Nowata deputy, George Lawson, came down to the

*depot and I took them in the back room telling them what I
had done and how it looked to me. They agreed.*

The conjecture by Bristow is not totally convincing in it-
self, I don't believe it would hold up in a court hearing. We
do know that Lawson and Bill Smith did meet with Ike Rogers and that Rogers was given a new deputy U.S. marshal
commission on January 10, 1895. Clint Scales, mentioned by
Bristow, was a local Cherokee Freedman who assisted Rogers in the capture of Cherokee Bill.

Smith and Lawson were aware that Cherokee Bill did
come to Rogers' home to meet Maggie Glass. Also, they did
promise Rogers a share of the reward money with the capture of Cherokee Bill. Did they also hold the collusion theo-
ry of Bristow over Rogers' head for his cooperation? We will
never really know, but one thing for certain Cherokee Bill
and Ike Rogers were on friendly terms.

The story by Bristow might shed light on how the fed-
eral officers were able to force Ike Rogers, a former depu-
ty U.S. marshal, to assist with the capture of Cherokee Bill.
Yes, he would consider the reward, but more importantly if
Bristow's story is true, they could point to direct evidence,
showing collusion between Rogers and Cherokee Bill. Pos-
sibly, Rogers was given a choice, he took the high road. Also,
Rogers would be reappointed as a deputy U.S. marshal by
U.S. Marshal George Crump due to his help in capturing
Cherokee Bill. Records at the Fort Smith National Historic
Site (NPS) show Rogers received a new commission on Jan-
uary 10, 1895, a few days before Cherokee Bill was captured.

On January 12, 1895, Bill Cook was arrested in New Mexico by Sheriff Charley Perry of Chavez County and Sheriff
Tom D. Love of Borden County, Texas. Cook was taken to
the federal jail in Fort Smith, Arkansas, by the lawmen.

Chapter Nine

The Capture

The scheme to catch Cherokee Bill was plotted by U.S. Marshal Crump and Deputy U.S. Marshals W. C. "Bill" Smith and George Lawson, the two veteran officers most dedicated to bringing Cherokee Bill in dead or alive. The plan was to invite Roger's niece Maggie Glass to his home on her seventeenth birthday, January 29. Maggie was the niece of Ike's wife. He would also invite Cherokee Bill over for the celebration.

Rogers could depend on Clint Scales, who worked as a federal posseman on many occasions, to assist with the capture. Crump would station deputies Smith and Lawson at Nowata to await the arrival of Rogers with their prisoner, dead or alive. Scales was to be watching the cabin, and when he saw Bill arrive, he was to drop in casually and spend the night. They were to catch Cherokee Bill off guard and capture him, in return for which Ike Rogers and Scales were each to get a third of the reward money. Maggie Glass would be the unsuspecting bait to trap Bill. She readily consented to the visit that was arranged by her uncle.

On Tuesday afternoon, January 29, 1895, Ike Rogers saw Bill ride towards the house of a man named Jackson, and he sent his boy to tell Bill he wanted to see him. Shortly after dark the outlaw came to Rogers' house, dismounted, and entered. Several hours after he arrived, Clint Scales put in an appearance. Not one moment elapsed that the outlaw

The parents of Maggie Glass, Looney and Mary Glass (both standing).

was not on his guard, prepared to use his Winchester. Maggie, also, was suspicious of Rogers, and she warned Bill to leave, but Bill refused to run away, telling the girl he would show Rogers how long it would take him to commit murder, his plan being to let Rogers make the first move, then shoot him in his tracks.

Rogers, in turn, was acting the part of the generous host; he watched for an opportunity to strike a deadly blow that would give him part of the promised reward. He treated the outlaw with the greatest kindness and managed to gain his confidence somewhat and urged him to stay all night. Once he suggested that the outlaw lay down his Winchester. "That's something I never do," replied the desperado. Next,

Rogers offered him some whiskey doctored with morphine which he obtained from Deputy Smith, but Cherokee Bill refused to drink.

According to Rogers' account, Bill and Maggie were alone for some time before supper. When all sat down to the table, Bill kept his rifle on his lap. Supper over, the three men played cards for small stakes. Bill sat with his back to the wall. While the game was in progress, Rogers watched for an opportunity to overpower him, but Cherokee was observant of every movement. The weapons of the would-be captors were necessarily kept from sight as they didn't want to give Bill an excuse for a fight. Maggie grew weary of waiting for her lover and went to bed with Mrs. Rogers, her aunt.

The men played cards until 4:00 a.m. For hours, Scales and Rogers had been watching Cherokee Bill like hawks, but hunted animal that he was, he watched them just as warily, as though he knew what was on their minds. When they were ready to turn in, Scales bedded down on the floor and Cherokee Bill got into bed with Rogers, his rifle on the blanket at his side. Rogers lay awake for some time, hoping to catch Cherokee asleep, but whenever he would move the other would instantly rise in bed, ready to use his Winchester.

At breakfast time it began to appear as if the plan was not working. After eating, Ike sent Maggie to a neighbor's house, a quarter of a mile away, to buy a couple of chickens. The day was cold; it was January but there was no snow on the ground. From what followed, it would appear that it made no difference whether Maggie was in the cabin or ten miles away; she had innocently served her purpose and there was nothing further she could do.

The *Ohio Democrat* newspaper of New Philadelphia, Ohio, reported on the capture on February 9, 1895:

CHEROKEE BILL AT
LAST TAKEN IN BY A COLORED MAN.

W. C. Smith, Deputy Marshal, has distinguished himself again in effecting the capture of Cherokee Bill, the companion of Bill Cook, in the Indian Territory during the last five months. Cherokee Bill's headquarters were known to be Nowata, IT. Smith made arrangements with Ike Rogers and Clint Scales, colored citizens living near there, to wait for Bill. The outlaw stopped at Roger's house and went to bed with Rogers without any fear of a trap. Wednesday morning, after breakfast, Rogers stepped behind Bill, seized a club and struck him over the head knocking him down. Bill boasts that he had killed fifteen men and admits the killing of Station Agent Dick Richards at Nowata last summer. He also confessed to killing his brother-in-law at the same place some weeks ago.

The following is an interview given by Ike Rogers to Frank Weaver, court reporter for the weekly *Fort Smith Elevator:*

. . . I had been instructed by Colonel Crump to get him alive, if possible, and I didn't want to kill him if I couldn't get him in any other way. Scales and I had our guns hidden where we could get them in a hurry but we didn't want to give them any show to fight. After breakfast, we talked along for some time and he began to talk of leaving. He and Scales and I sat in front of the open fireplace. I knowed that we had to make a break on him pretty soon and I was afraid the girl would take a hand in it when the trouble began, so I gave her a dollar to buy some chickens at a neighbor's as

to get her out of the way. I also sent my boys away as I had not told them of my plans. Bill finally took a notion that he wanted to smoke and he took some paper and tobacco from his pocket and rolled a cigarette. He had no match, so he stooped over towards the fireplace, to light it, and turned his head away from me for an instant. That was my chance and I took it. There was a fire stick lying on the floor near me and I grabbed it up and struck him across the back of the head. I must have hit him hard enough to kill an ordinary man but it only knocked him down. Scales and I then jumped on him but he let out one yell and got on his feet. My wife grabbed Bill's Winchester and we three tussled on the floor, full twenty minutes. I thought once I would have to kill him, his great strength, with his 180 pounds weight, being too much for me and Scales, but finally we got a pair of handcuffs on him. He promised me money and horses, all I wanted. Then he cursed. We put him in a wagon and Scales rode with him and I went on horseback, and started for Nowata. On the way Cherokee broke his handcuffs and grabbed at Scales' gun and Scales had to fall out of the wagon to keep from losing his Winchester, while I kept Cherokee covered with my shotgun. At Nowata, we turned him over to Bill Smith and George Lawson.

Ike Rogers gave another interview to a reporter in Fort Smith, Arkansas, who worked for the *St. Louis Post-Dispatch* newspaper detailing the capture of Cherokee Bill. The same article ran in the *Eufaula Indian Journal* on February 8, 1895:

. . . Cherokee Bill staid (sic) at my house all night, and Scales and I had determined to take him dead or alive, but alive if possible. I had been instructed by Col. Crump to capture him alive if possible, but to capture him at all haz-

ards.

Scales and I had our guns handy, but did not want to fight, as Bill never raises his gun to his shoulder, but shoots from the hip and the chances are he would have got both of us. Bill finally took a notion to smoke . . . He did not have a match, so he stooped over toward the fireplace to light it, turning his head from me for only a moment.

My chance had come at last, there was a fire stick lying on the floor near me . . . I hit him hard enough to kill an ordinary man, but it only knocked him down. Scales jumped for him, but with an inhuman yell he was on his feet . . . Bill, Scales and myself scuffled on the floor fully twenty minutes. I thought once I would have to kill him, but finally got the handcuffs on him . . . We then in a wagon and started for Nowata.

On the way he broke the handcuffs and grabbed Scales gun, Scales had to fall out of the wagon to keep Bill from getting his Winchester. I kept Bill covered with my shotgun, the only weapon on earth that Cherokee was afraid of.

Later in the same article, Cherokee Bill was interviewed:

I would not be here now if it had not been for men who claimed to be my friends; you boys did not do me right, sure you didn't, he said turning to Deputy W. C. Smith . . .

I am 19 years old; and was born and raised in the Cherokee Nation. I have been on the scout for several years, and was never caught before. I would not have been caught this time if I had listened to the girl. She told me I had better not stay at that house, but I thought I could whip both of them if I got a show, but they knocked me down with a club, instead of going after guns.

Did you ever see any of the marshals while they were

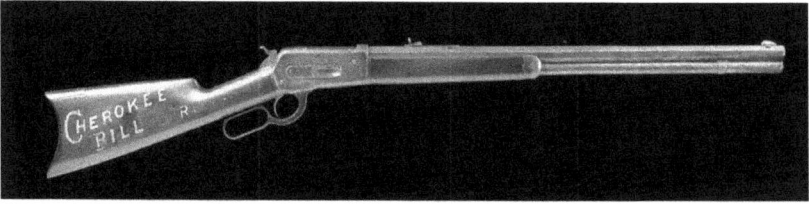

Cherokee Bill's cherished 1886 Winchester rifle, which he kept close at all times, even in bed.

after you?

No, I have never saw any of them except when smoke was coming out of my gun. If they will just put me on the prairie, I can whip any five, yes and ten deputy marshals in the Territory. Those fellows did a brave act, but they are cowards, and they know it . . .

At Nowata, deputies Smith and Lawson took charge of the prisoner, Cherokee Bill was manacled and placed in an Arkansas Valley Railroad cattle car. Many people flocked around after the news got out and people came and stared through the boards of the car as if he was a circus attraction. It was said that the famous Oklahoman Will Rogers was there as a young man in the crowd in Nowata when Cherokee Bill was brought to the train station for his journey to Fort Smith.

Deputy Smith telegraphed Marshal Crump at Fort Smith, "Will be there on morning train 266 with Cherokee Bill. Did not hurt him." There was complete disbelief in Fort Smith that the notorious young outlaw had been captured.

A large crowd of Indian Territory citizens waited to get a glimpse of Bill as the train moved through Claremore. At Wagoner in the Creek Nation, Deputy U.S. Marshals Zeke and Dick Crittenden joined Lawson and Smith as additional guards. It was at this location that Cherokee Bill was brought

Cherokee Bill and his captors at Nowata.

out of the car in leg irons, and the captors and guards along with Bill were photographed by Wagoner photographer E. D. MacFee. The photo shows Ike Rogers, Clint Scales, Deputy U.S. Marshal Smith and Dick and Zeke Crittenden, with Cherokee Bill, his feet in chains, as the centerpiece. This became one of the very few images of Cherokee Bill.

In the photo, Cherokee Bill refused to let Ike Rogers stand beside him, and threw his right arm around Dick Crittenden, saying, "Here is a fellow that stood up and fought me like a man [at Halfway House]; I will have my picture taken with him."

At the same time Bill reached for Crittenden's pistol, which the guard prevented from happening. Later, Bill said some of the officers "would have worn away wooden overcoats," and Rogers "would not have reached Fort Smith to receive any of the reward," if he had been successful in getting the pistol.

At Fort Smith, Cherokee Bill came up for arraignment before Judge Parker, charged with the murder of Ernest Melton. Bill's mother, Ellen Lynch, had retained the most famous trial lawyer in Fort Smith. It is believed J. Warren Reed took the case because he had a running feud with Judge Parker. The trial was certain to attract tremendous attention, perhaps more than any heard by the Fort Smith court, which it did. With the evidence against the notorious outlaw so strong, Reed undoubtedly expected Parker to run roughshod over the defendant's legal rights. Sufficiently pushed, he might overstep the rules of jurisprudence flagrantly enough to convince the U.S. Supreme Court that a fair trial could not be had in the Fort Smith court, which Reed had been contending for years.

Cherokee Bill was placed on the same tier as Bill Cook in the jail. J. E. Kelly, the founder of Kellyville, Creek Nation, Indian Territory, and was the postmaster, store owner of that town came to visit Bill in jail. Mr. Kelly spent a portion of his early life on the frontier and was a cowboy in the 1870s, in Wyoming and Nebraska. He knew the Cook brothers and Cherokee Bill intimately, long before they became outlaws. Kelly described an incident that showed Bill's agility and love of the gun:

Cherokee Bill was game as a hornet, and a true friend but a bitter enemy. He was quick and active and always wide awake. He was not shamming, he was an outlaw in good earnest. I saw him at Fort Smith shortly after his arrest. George Lawson, who figured in his arrest, asked me up to the jail to see him. He brought Bill out to have his photograph taken. Bill was "hot" and was crying with madness when he appeared. Lawson said, "Bill, quit your crying; here is Kelly who has come to see you; why don't you ask him about some of your

Deputy U.S. Marshal George Lawson who was Cherokee Bill's executioner.

old friends?" Bill, who up to this time had not raised his eyes, looked up quickly, and as he saw me he smiled through his tears and grabbed my hand exclaimed, "Hello, old friend! I never thought you would see me down here. I thought you might see me all shot to -, but I never thought you would see me here." He was handed a beautiful Winchester, the property of Post-office inspector Houk, and was asked to pose for his picture. The gun was empty. Bill's eyes snapped with the old time fire; he took a position as if he had been surprised; he brought the gun into position and every nerve seemed on alert. Oh! How he would have loved to be out in the jail yard with the gun full of cartridges. After the photographer had finished, Bill fondled the gun and asked several questions about it; he seemed loath to give it up, and before returning it he worked the lever and the trigger until it clicked like a sewing machine. It was the wonder of all the deputy marshals, how he could shoot so fast. Bill said he knew his rapid firing was not always accurate, and he might not always hit his target, but he would shoot so —fast that he would "rattle" his antagonist "so he could not hit me.

Chapter Ten

Fort Smith Trial

Cherokee Bill was indicted for the murder of Ernest Melton on February 8, 1895. He pled not guilty at the arraignment before Judge Isaac C. Parker, who then set his trial for the last week in February. Parker wanted to move this trial as fast as he could. Cherokee Bill was indicted for the robbery of the store and post office of Donaldson and Foster at Watova, Cherokee Nation, on February 14.

On February 15, he was indicted for the October 9, 1894, American Express Company robbery at Chouteau, Cherokee Nation. On February 23, a petit jury returned guilty verdicts, and Cherokee Bill remained in the federal jail, bail denied, with sentencing in both cases to be decided at a later date.

The Melton murder trial began at noon, on February 26, 1895, with Judge Parker presiding. The trial pitted District Attorney James F. Read against the most successful defense attorney in Fort Smith, J. Warren Reed. Cherokee Bill's mother had been successful in attaining the best attorney she could find to defend her son. Many of the defense attorneys in Fort Smith felt it was a game of bragging rights to go up against the federal prosecutors and Judge Parker and win a case.

Reed had come to Fort Smith in 1886 to defend a noted case. He was born in West Virginia and had lived in Ohio and California before settling in Fort Smith, Arkansas. Reed was

Judge Isaac Parker—1896

attracted by the large volume of business in the federal court in the border town. Reed had been successful in winning his cases or reducing the sentences in 130 prior cases before he took Cherokee Bill as a client. Also, with Cherokee Bill being the most noted outlaw in the history of the Indian Territory it would bring more attention to the defense attorney's resume and skills to take this highly visible case.

Reed realized right off that his defense would have to entail establishing an alibi for the whereabouts of Cherokee Bill at the time of the Melton murder. Reed was able to get a half a dozen friends, including Bill's brother, Clarence, to place Bill's location as Fort Gibson at the time the crime occurred. This was near 100 miles from Lenapah. Testimony was then given that Bill traveled to a location six miles east of Claremore, then he was seen riding toward Tulsa. Bill visited a friend eight miles west of Tulsa. Then Bill was seen at a location five miles southwest of Tulsa, and finally had dinner with friends on November 10, three miles south of Red Fork. Attorney Reed, therefore said that Goldsby had been, "Seventy-five miles from Lenapah, rendering it impossible that the defendant could have been at the place at the time

The Fort Smith Federal Courthouse and on left the county courthouse *circa* 1890-1896.

of said robbery and murder, or participated therein."

A Cherokee Freedman took the stand and testified that he knew Jim French and Cherokee Bill, and that he had been in Lenapah at the time of the murder and Goldsby was not present. He said that Jim French was the person that killed Melton, and the man doing the shooting in front of the store was the Verdigris Kid. By the time of this trial Jim French had been killed by a posse and the Verdigris Kid was still at large.

The prosecution tried to weaken the alibi by saying the Cook Gang was known to ride sixty miles at night if necessary to elude the law. John Schufeldt and customers who were at the store positively identified Cherokee Bill as the man who shot Melton. The brother of Melton, W. S. Melton, showed the .45-90 cartridge case which was ejected and a bullet that had lodged in the wall of the restaurant after passing through his brother's head.

Cherokee Freedman Ben Vann testified that Cherokee Bill said at Ike Rogers' home, "I didn't intend to kill Melton, only shot to scare him."

Deputy U.S. Marshal Bill Smith testified that while bringing Cherokee Bill from Nowata on the train, he said, "I don't see how they can prove the killing on me, for there were others shooting besides me."

Arguments in the case began at noon, February 26, 1895, and lasted until 10 p.m. that night. Judge Parker instructed the jury the next morning, occupying only fifteen minutes in his charge. The jury returned a fast verdict within a few minutes after retiring for deliberations. Cherokee Bill smiled when the verdict "guilty," was read, but his mother and sister, who attended the trial, wept loudly.

Cherokee Bill responded to his mother and sister's remonstrations, "What's the matter with you? I'm not a dead man yet, by a long ways," he loudly proclaimed to the women. Over at the federal jail later that afternoon, Cherokee Bill was engaged in a game of poker with Bill Cook and several others, as if nothing had happened.

On Saturday morning, April 13, Cherokee Bill was brought before Judge Parker to be sentenced in the murder of Ernest Melton. To discourage a large crowd, the sentencing had been made known to only a few. Cherokee Bill was accompanied by Lawyer Reed, who alleged five errors on which he felt the outlaw deserved a new trial. Judge Parker over-ruled Reed's application, and Reed announced his desire to appeal. Judge Parker recognized that privilege, then addressed Cherokee Bill in part said:

> *From the evidence in the case there can be no doubt of*
> *your guilt. That evidence shows a killing of the most brutal*

and wicked character. . . . Melton was the innocent, unof-
fending victim of the savage brutality which prompted the
robbery and murder. . . . From the information that has
come to me, this murder is one of three committed by you
and the others were equally as wicked and unprovoked. . . .

Happily for the peace of the country, the whole of the
band in which you belonged has been broken up . . . killed
by officers while in the act of committing crimes, or in re-
sisting arrests, and this has all happened to them in less
than a year.

Now it behooves you to prepare to meet your fate. You
must reflect on your past life, and fully comprehend its wick-
edness, and the injuries that your acts have done others. . .
. You must seek forgiveness from the author of all mercy,
the good God, whose government is so much higher than
human government that he can forgive the worst crimes.
Then I ask you to consider that no one can doubt the justice
of your conviction, or the certainty of your guilt, so you can
enter upon a new existence with your sins, wickedness and
crime behind you. Do everything you can to accomplish this
end, and lose not a moment's time. . . .

It is the duty of this court to pass the sentence upon
you, which under the law follows such a conviction, and
which public justice demands. . . .

Judge Parker asked Goldsby if he had anything to say,
he replied, "No Sir." June 25, 1895, was the day set for execution.

Lawyer Reed found fourteen "manifest errors to the
prejudice and great damage" to himself and his client. On
April 29, Reed appealed to the U.S. Supreme Court.

Meanwhile Bill Cook was being removed from the Fort

Smith federal jail and moved with nineteen other prisoners to the prison in Albany, New York, on April 30. At a stop at Springfield, Missouri, Cook talked to the crowd at the railroad station from his window in the prison car and offered pictures of himself for sale. Cook was asked by a reporter if he thought Crawford Goldsby would be executed on June 25, he replied, "No bars can hold Cherokee."

With Reed's appeal of the conviction, Judge Parker set July 25 as the new date for the hanging of Cherokee Bill. Reed also appealed to President Cleveland for a commutation. President Cleveland agreed to look at the evidence and to examine the matter.

When June 25, 1895, arrived, the day first named as Cherokee Bill's execution day, his appeal was still in the hands of the Supreme Court, and Judge Parker issued a stay of execution to give the Supreme Court time to act.

Chapter Eleven

Cherokee Bill's Last Stand

Before Cherokee Bill arrived in the Fort Smith federal jail, Henry Starr had preceded him there. They were friends from the Cherokee Nation and Cherokee Bill found a kindred spirit in the jail. Starr, born December 2, 1873, at Fort Gibson, Cherokee Nation, was a son of Hop Starr, a half-blood Cherokee. His mother was only a quarter-blood, which made Henry more white than Indian, although Henry always felt more Indian than white. His grandfather was Tom Starr, the infamous Cherokee who terrorized the Indian Territory prior to the Civil War. His uncle was Sam Starr, who married the famous Belle Starr of Indian Territory legend.

Henry was courteous, acquired before his end an education which gave him an almost conversational grace, liked to read good literature, and was a pleasant companion. Throughout his life he displayed a remarkable ability to make friends and keep their friendship.

In later years, Henry wrote about growing up in the Indian Territory:

I had always looked upon the Indian as supreme and the white renters as trash who moved from year to year in covered wagons with many dogs and tow-headed kids peeping out from behind every wagon-bow, and who, at the very best, made only a starving crop. The Indian landowner was looked up to by his white renters, and always treated with

Federal guards at Fort Smith, AR., circa 1890s.

courtesy and respect. But the years have brought about a change, the white man holds power, and the same hypocritical renter had grown arrogant and insulting; whenever the Indian, and especially the full-blood in Oklahoma, is an outcast in his own country, and it is with a feeling of sadness and apprehension that I think of his future. Broken treaties, misplaced confidence and insult that made him lose interest in life. I have more white blood than Indian, and with my knowledge of both races, I fervently wish that every drop in my veins was red!

Starr's first run-in with the law was in June of 1891. Starr while working for a cattle ranch said he was in a buggy on his way to Nowata when met a person he knew who was riding horseback on his way to a Delaware Indian payment. The friend had a large bag and asked Henry could he take it to the payment grounds which were close by.

After about two miles Henry was met by two deputy

U.S. marshals with drawn guns wanting to know what was in the bag, which Henry said he had no idea. In searching the bag the deputies found two bottles of illegal whiskey. The deputies arrested Henry for trafficking in illegal whiskey. He was taken to the federal court in Muskogee.

The rancher Henry was working for bonded him out and advised him to plead guilty instead of fighting a long drawn out trial. One of the deputies at his hearing said he didn't think Henry was a whiskey peddler and believed his story that he didn't know what was in the bag. The judge fined Henry $100 for the offense of introducing, Henry paid it and returned to Nowata.

The second run in with the law occurred in October of 1891 while he was working for the Robert's ranch in the Cherokee Nation as a cowboy. Starr found two horses that had strayed in to the ranch's pasture. He informed other ranchers in the area of the horses. Charles Eaton later claimed one of the horses and was pleased that horse was well taken care of and offered to pay Henry for his troubles.

A few months later in December Henry was met in Nowata by a deputy U.S. marshal with a warrant for his arrest for horse theft. This time Henry was taken to the Fort Smith federal jail. Eaton later pretty much repeated Starr's story at the court hearing and Starr was released from custody.

After his first two brushes with the law, Starr found a friend in Albert Dodge, a rancher living near Nowata, who gave him a job as a cowboy. Starr was a good cowhand, until 1892, when he was arrested again for horse theft. This time he was released on bond, furnished by his cousin Kale Starr and J. C. Harris, the tribal chief of the Cherokees.

The same day his case was called in Fort Smith, Henry was deep in the Osage country. Along with some other shady characters, Henry executed robberies in the Cherokee Nation and was now seriously "on the scout." (On the scout in the territory meant a felon was on the run from the law). Starr had now gained a reputation in the outlaw country.

When Starr failed to appear for his trial in Fort Smith, his bondsman, upset under the forfeiture of $2000, offered a reward for his capture. At the same time, Stephen Wheeler, U.S. Commissioner for the Western District of Arkansas federal court, issued a warrant for his arrest.

Henry C. Dickey, the express company detective investigating the Nowata robbery, of which Starr was a suspect, had possession of the warrant for Starr's arrest. Dickey was able to get a deputy U.S. marshal commission for Floyd Wilson, a long-time lawman of the Indian Territory, to assist with the hunt and arrest of Starr.

On December 12, 1892, Dicky and Wilson picked up Starr's trail near Lenapah. They proceeded south by rail, and at dusk arrived at Dodge's "XU" Ranch, eight miles from Nowata, where it had been reported the gang was hiding out. Dodge denied the gang was personally known by him, but admitted he had seen Starr ride past his place several times.

The following day, as they sat at dinner with the ranchman's family, Dodge galloped in from checking his spread on the ranch and informed them he had just seen Starr ride past again. Wilson ran to the stable, mounted a horse, already saddled and bridled, on which Dodge had just returned and rode off in the direction in which Starr had been seen. Dickey was delayed several minutes by saddling up a fresh mount. Wilson pressed on ahead of the detective to take the fugitive alone. Wilson had obtained his gung-ho spirit from earlier serving as a deputy U.S. marshal where on many occasions he rode with the legendary black deputy Bass Reeves. He found Starr in an opening on Wolf Creek.

Wilson ordered Starr to halt and rode up to within twenty-five or thirty feet of Starr.

"You hold up!" called Starr, who made no further effort to flee. Wilson then sprang from his horse, threw his rifle to his shoulder, and fired over the outlaw's head to frighten him.

Starr had been standing with his rifle in his hands, holding the muzzle down. Upon Wilson's shooting, Starr returned the fire and continued to fire rapidly. Wilson fell, badly wounded. As he lay there, too weak to lift the six-shooter he had drawn; Starr calmly strode forward and fired another bullet into Wilson's heart. The rifle was so close that the blaze spouting from its muzzle scorched the officer's clothing.

Legendary African American lawman, Bass Reeves.

Dickey had failed to reach his companion before the shooting started. Starr escaped and Dickey took Wilson's body by train to

Coffeyville, Kansas. Starr was now wanted for killing a deputy U.S. marshal, a hanging offense.

Starr led a gang in the robbery of the People's Bank at Bentonville, Arkansas, on June 5, 1893. In July of 1893, Henry was arrested in Colorado Springs, Colorado, by local lawmen with his girlfriend trying to hide out. Federal lawmen from Fort Smith took Starr back to Arkansas to stand trial. Henry was nineteen-years of age at the time.

At his trial in Fort Smith, fourteen separate indictments, including one for the murder of Floyd Wilson, were lodged against him. He was convicted of that murder and Judge Parker sentenced him to hang by the neck until dead. The date of execution was for February 20, 1895. Henry was fortunate enough to get a new trial set up the U.S. Supreme Court; he was an inmate in the federal jail when Cherokee Bill made his appearance.

J. D. Berry, former deputy sheriff of Franklin County, Arkansas, was head jailer at the Fort Smith federal jail and was as competent as any who served during Judge Parker's tenure. There were more than 200 convicts in the jail in the spring of 1895, and hardly a day passed that there was not some scheme afoot for a single escape or a wholesale run for freedom. There were several prisoners who managed to elude jailers and escape from the new jail wing that was built in 1888.

On July 10, he ordered a search of the entire prison. In Cherokee Bill's cell the guards found nine .45 cartridges, and in the bathroom on Murderer's Row they found a .45 revolver, fully loaded, hidden in a bucket of lime.

Sherman Vann, a black trusty serving ninety days for larceny, was suspected. Vann admitted carrying in the lime, but if the weapon and ammunition were hidden there, he never knew it. Cherokee Bill's cohorts denied that they knew where the weapon came from. Henry Starr was one of the first questioned by Berry, but most of the guards doubted he had anything to do with it.

During the week following, it was again whispered throughout the city that Cherokee Bill would kill somebody in the jail. Although Berry and his guards remained alert, they foolishly allowed him the freedom of the Row during the day, the same as the other prisoners, without leg irons, although the newspapers gave warning of the danger. The jail guards also failed to discover a second revolver that had been smuggled into his cell. Cherokee Bill had hidden the pistol in the wall behind a loose stone. The inside half of the stone had been broken off and the whitewashed end replaced.

At 7 p.m. on the evening of July 26, turnkey Campbell Eoff (pronounced Ofe) and guard Lawrence Keating entered Murderers' Row. The guards at the jail usually were relieved by the night guards at 6 p.m., and 6:15p.m. was the time for locking the cells on each of the three floors. Owing to the long days and hot weather, the prisoners were allowed to remain in the corridors until near 7 p.m.

It was the responsibility of Eoff and Keating, who guarded the lower tier of cells in the daytime, to "ring" the prisoners in for the night. Night guards Will Lawson, Bras Parker, and William McConnell had just come on duty and were sitting on the ground outside, ten feet from the corridor entrance and the stairway to the jailer's office. Captain Berry had been gone about ten minutes.

Two rows of cells ran north and south of each side of the inner corridor, or "bullpen." The whole inner part of the jail was built of chilled steel, the doors of cross-barred steel, and the corridor walls of steel bars crossed as open grates. Every prisoner had his own cell, and when the gong sounded, each was to go to his proper cell and close his door behind him. Then a guard at the entrance threw a lever, dropping a long bar or "brake," intended to fasten the closed cell doors on either side at the top.

It was Eoff's job, after the lever was pulled, to enter the corridor and lock each door separately. It was a comparatively safe procedure, but there was always the chance that prisoners might hide at the rear of the cage or otherwise deceive the unarmed turnkey. To lessen the danger, Keating, wearing his pistol, walked along outside the cage to make sure each man was in his cell and had closed his door in order that the brake work properly.

The brake on either row could be opened, however, by a broomstick or similar instrument in the hands of a prisoner at the north end of the tier. In compliance with a concerted movement to capture the jail, it was thrown open on the west tier, where Cherokee Bill and his associates were confined, while Eoff and Keating were attending the cells on the east side. As the turnkey passed around the south end and started locking the doors of the west row, Keating kept pace outside the corridor. Cherokee Bill's door, like the others, was free to be pushed open, and he calmly waited with a revolver ready.

Cherokee Bill's cell was "No. 20" and was the third from the south end. Adjoining his cell on the south was one occupied by Dennis Davis, a mentally challenged black man convicted of murdering one Solomon Blackwell. The keyhole in the lock of his door had been stuffed with paper. When Eoff inserted the key it lodged in the lock, and he remarked to Keating, "There's something wrong here."

Keating walked closer. At that instant, the door of Cherokee Bill's cell was pushed open and Bill leaped out across the short space, shoved the muzzle of a revolver through the bars at Keating, and shouted, "Throw up, and give me that pistol!"

Instead of obeying, Keating with a great deal of courage reached for his own revolver. Instantly, Cherokee Bill's

Prison guard, Larry Keating

weapon was in action, and Keating staggered back, fatally wounded.

Eoff, who was unarmed, turned when the shot was fired and ran up the corridor, while Cherokee Bill stepped out of his cell and fired at him twice, but missed both times. George Pearce one of the ringleaders in the plot, jumped from his cell and joined the chase, brandishing a broken table leg for a club. This perhaps saved Eoff's life, as Bill could not shoot squarely at him without endangering Pearce.

Eoff took refuge in the doorway of the front cage. But for the prompt appearance of federal guards Will Lawson, Bras Parker and McConnell at the jail door, he would have undoubtedly have lost his life. The guards opened fire and drove Cherokee Bill and Pearce back to the south end of the corridor.

When the shooting started, bedlam broke out in the prison. Convicts howled and threw their weight against the bars. From some of the cells still unlocked, men made ready for a full-scale prison riot. Above the frenzied yelling of the prisoners, and the shouts of officers ordering them back into their cells, the explosion of firearms rang out again and again, as Cherokee Bill tried to drive the guards from the gate and they replied in like fashion. Smoke so filled the corridor that it was almost impossible to see, which was the reason why more people were not killed or wounded.

Out of the smoke suddenly appeared a dreadful figure: Lawrence Keating, still carrying his revolver, the blood cascading from his body, his face drawn and pale like the ghost of a man already dead. Dead he really was, except for the effort of will that kept him staggering on, carrying the weapon which the murderer behind might have used, until he collapsed by the gate, gasped, "I'm killed," and died.

Now Heck Bruner, a deputy U.S. marshal, one of Cherokee Bill's most hated foes, came up with a shotgun and blasted with it down the corridor. The "scatter gun" would have done some serious damage, if it could have been brought into play sooner. But when Bruner fired, Cherokee Bill and all the other prisoners had already retreated into their cells, so that the buck shot whined and rattled down the passageway without finding a living target.

Then there began a sniping gun fight. Cherokee Bill, having reloaded his revolver, fired at random from his cell, never putting out his head. Every time he fired, he gobbled. It was an uncanny, though familiar, sound in the Cherokee Nation, half between the bark of a coyote and the throaty cry of a turkey cock—the same cry that the infamous Cherokee Ned Christie used while under siege. When a Cherokee Indian "gobbled" it meant sure death to someone within hearing range, as much a threat to kill as if spoken in so many words.

For fifteen minutes Cherokee Bill gobbled and fired at every form and shadow he could see. He fired at Jim Shannon and another citizen as they carried Keating's lifeless form outside. The place was fumed with the stench of gunpowder. Only this and the fact that the officers were able to keep Bill confined in his cell prevented a dozen men from being slain.

It was always claimed by the officers that just after the first shot, the lever which fastened the cell doors at the top was thrown, thus liberating all the cells which had not been locked with a key. Who was responsible for this act was never settled further than that it was someone near the north end. Henry Starr was suspected of the deed, but none saw him in the act.

The excitement rapidly spread to the city. In an incredibly short time, police and scores of citizens armed themselves with Winchesters, shotguns, and revolvers and hastened to help the guards. Marshal Crump arrived from his home in the suburbs and took personal charge of the situation.

Firearms were at every step. The prisoners, for the most part, were badly frightened and had taken refuge beneath their bunks or huddled in the corner of their cells. On the outside of the cell blocks were twenty or more men, all armed to the teeth. Captain Berry vainly tried to induce Cherokee Bill to surrender his weapon. A steady refusal was the only response.

It was at this moment that Henry Starr stepped unforgettably into the picture. He had been sentenced to hang for the murder of peace officer Floyd Wilson, but his lawyer had appealed the case, and he was awaiting a decision on the appeal in his cell in the Fort Smith federal jail. Now he managed to get the attention of one of the guards, and made this proposal. "If you'll keep the men who are watching the corridor from shooting at me, I'll go into Cherokee Bill's cell and get his gun for you."

Starr knew Bill from their association in the Cook Gang. After a consultation was held, the guards agreed not to fire. Released from his cell, young Starr walked steadily down the corridor to the cell occupied by cornered Cherokee Bill.

Starr described what happened next:

. . . I pledged myself to get Bill's gun if (Crump) would give me his word of honor that he would not shoot him when disarmed, which he did. I went at once to Bill's cell and told him that he could not possibly get out – that he might be able to kill a few more guards, but that would avail nothing, and to take my advice and give his gun to me, which he did, loaded all around. I walked to the end of the corridor and handed the gun to the guards.

Starr went on to tell newspaper reporters later:

I said, 'Bill, you can't get out . . . Why kill a lot of people? He replied, 'I'm going to kill every white man in sight. I'll kill you if you come any closer.' If Bill had one soft spot, it was his devotion to his mother. I said, 'Your mother don't want you to kill more than you have already. Why hurt her more? My plea to give up his pistol for her sake touched him. 'Take it, he said and handed over the gun.

It was that simple.

The officers entered the corridor, covering Cherokee Bill with shotguns and Winchesters. A thorough search of his cell turned up a little tobacco sack filled with .38 cartridges. Then he was handcuffed, chained, and locked back inside. George Pearce, found hiding in his cell, was also chained and locked up, and the jail was cleared of spectators.

Cherokee Bill felt remorse at having to shoot Larry Keating. He felt Keating was going to shoot him if he hadn't shot in self-defense. Bill went on to say, "Damn a man who won't fight for his liberty!"

No less than one hundred shots were fired in the attempted jail break. Most of the gunfire came from the guards trying to quell the escape.

The deputy U.S. marshals and guards worked until midnight dispersing the crowds and discouraging mob violence. District Attorney James F. Read mingled quietly with the people, assuring them the case would be vigorously prosecuted and the crime would not go unavenged. Nothing else was talked about in public places for a week, while Cherokee Bill became sullen and morose and for several days almost entirely refused food.

Chapter Twelve

The Execution

At the time of Keating's murder, Judge Isaac C. Parker was in St. Louis. Not in very good health, he knew that very soon his beloved court, in which he had ruled virtually as a personification of fate for so many years, would be abolished. The iron-clad murder case against Cherokee Bill was like a stimulant to him. On Thursday following the crime, the judge left St. Louis and returned to Fort Smith for the purpose of convening court and calling the grand jury together, that they might return an indictment against Cherokee Bill for the murder of Keating.

The autumn term of court began on August 5. The trial docket, seldom taken up until October, was so heavy that Judge Parker canceled his vacation, which he usually took at that time of year. For the first time in the court's history, the petit and grand juries were empaneled on the opening day. There were twenty-four murder cases scheduled, and the grand jury added twenty more. The first case taken up was the killing of Keating.

An investigation was done in the conspiracy to foment a jail break that resulted in guard Keating's death. A grand jury was heavily involved in questioning Henry Starr, Sherman Vann, Edward and John Shelley, and Edward Shelley's wife Lu, all had been indicted as accessories to the murder. The Shelleys had been in the Fort Smith jail for escaping a jail in Oklahoma Territory and were captured near Checotah on February 3, and charged with intent to kill Deputy U.S. Marshal John McCann. Lu Shelley was thought to have brought the gun to the jail that the guards found on Murderers' Row on July 10. All parties pled not guilty to the charges. Lu Shelley was released on bail.

Cherokee Bill made an affidavit that neither Henry Starr, the Shelleys nor Sherman Vann had anything to do with bringing any weapons into the jail that were used at the time Keating was killed. The government dropped the indictments against the Shelleys, Vann and Henry Starr.

For his courage in the Fort Smith jail, the death penalty against outlaw Henry Starr was lifted, and he was permitted to plead to a charge of manslaughter, for which he was sentenced to fifteen years in prison. He was pardoned by U.S. President Theodore Roosevelt after five years.

In Cherokee Bill's case, Judge Parker's charge to the grand jury was very forceful. Within half an hour, they returned an indictment against Bill, and at 1 p.m. in the afternoon, escorted by a dozen armed U.S. deputy marshals and a court bailiff with a heavy billy club, he was arraigned before Judge Parker. He entered a plea of not guilty, and Judge Parker set his trial for August 8.

On Thursday, August 8, Cherokee Bill was again brought into court in chains and under heavy guard. Never had the courtroom been attended by so many visitors making the standing room only available for those lucky enough to get in. His defense attorney, J. W. Reed, fought the case with every "hook and crook," from the beginning. He made a motion for continuance on grounds that public sentiment and prejudices of the people of Fort Smith would not allow his client to get a fair and impartial trial at that time, and filed a demurrer alleging that the court did not have jurisdiction because the killing had occurred in jail. Judge Parker ruled that "there is no question as to the jurisdiction of the court in this case"; he became "highly indignant" that a fair and impartial trial could not be had in his court, and stated that "the allegations in the demurrer are wholly false and without foundation."

He ordered the panel of jurors called. Twelve men who lived no closer than forty miles to Fort Smith were chosen. He questioned each man closely and satisfied that they were not prejudiced and could render a verdict in accordance with the law and evidence, pronounced them "qualified jurors."

The Cherokee Bill trial lasted three days, the prosecution being handled by District Attorney Read's able assistant, J. B. McDonough. In his closing arguments McDonough was quoted as saying:

To effect his capture, brave men risked their lives. Even after he had been placed within the prison walls . . . his ferocity prevented docility, and his only thought was to break away that he might return to the scene of bloodshed from which an outraged law had estranged him. . . .

Failing to work out his plan for escape, he deliberately, without a moment's hesitation, let out the life blood of a fellow human being, one who was beloved by all. . . . Then, nerved by the very scene of the fresh blood he spilled, he would add other terrors to the occasion by shooting even those who had come to carry away the dead body of the man he had ruthlessly slain. . . .

And now he comes here, with his hands steeped in human gore, with a long list of misdeed that should cause even the imps of hell to shudder . . . and ask mercy at your hand; mercy! For a series of crimes that knows no equal among men of the Nineteenth century; with his heart reeking with infamy, he pleads for mercy; this most ferocious of monsters, whose record is more atrocious than all the criminals who have hitherto stood before this bar; a creature whose very existence is a disgrace upon nature, a grievous burden to the atmosphere from which he draws his breath. . . ."

After closing arguments and verdict of the jury, which was guilty, Judge Parker sentenced Cherokee Bill to be hanged September 10, 1895. In his closing statements Judge Parker told Cherokee Bill:

Cherokee Bill . . . you revel in the destruction of human life. The many murders you have committed, and their reckless and wanton character, show you to be a human monster . . . You most wantonly and wickedly stole the life of a brave and true man . . . You most wickedly slew him in your mad attempt to evade the punishment justly due for your many murders. . . .

Keating . . . was a minister of peace; you were and are a minister of wickedness, of disorder, of crime, of murder . . . You have had a fair trial, notwithstanding the howls and shrieks to the contrary. There is no doubt of your guilt of a most wicked, foul and unprovoked murder, shocking to every good man and woman in the land.

I once before sentenced you to death for a horrible and wicked murder . . . I then appealed to your conscience by reminding you of your duty to your God and to your own soul. The appeal reached not to your conscience, for you answered it by committing another most foul and dastardly murder. I shall therefore say nothing to you on that line here and now.

You will now listen to the sentence of the law, which

is that you . . . be hanged by the neck until you are dead.
   May God who laws you have broken . . . have mercy
on your soul.

Again his case was appealed to the U.S. Supreme Court, and Parker granted another stay of execution. But on December 2, the Supreme Court affirmed the decision of the

S. G.   W. J. H.

7506--1895.   DEPARTMENT OF JUSTICE,
                                     WASHINGTON, D. C.

                                        May 9, 1896.

James F. Read, Esq.,
     U.S. Attorney,
          Fort Smith, Ark.
   Sir:
          There is pending on the docket of the Supreme Court the
   case of Crawford Goldsby, alias Cherokee Bill, vs. The United
   States, No. 728, an indictment for the murder of Lawrence Keating.
   The Supreme Court affirmed the judgment of the lower court in the
   former case No. 620, for the murder of Ernest Melton.   If the
   judgment in the case No. 620 has been carried out, and the plaintiff in error is now dead, the case No. 728 should be stricken from
   the docket of the Supreme Court.   Please advise me of the fact
   as to whether Goldsby has been executed or not.
                    Respectfully,

                              Holmes Conrad
                         Solicitor General.

The letter from the Department of Justice affirming Cherokee Bill's sentence following his appeal to the U.S. Supreme Court.

Fort Smith federal court in the Ernest Melton murder case. For the third and last time, Judge Parker sentenced Cherokee Bill to die on the gallows and fixed the date as St. Patrick's Day, March 17, 1896. There was "no avenue of escape left except executive clemency by the President, who was appealed to in vain. The U.S. President at that time was Grover Cleveland.

After his sentencing, Cherokee Bill was placed in solitary confinement. He did not seem to mind it, but he complained bitterly at his inability to obtain his mail. Under the rules, felons were not allowed to either receive or send mail when in solitary confinement, and letters addressed to Cherokee Bill were, of course, opened by jailer Berry and carefully read. One of the most persistent correspondents was a young African American girl, described as a mulatto, who lived in Indianapolis, Indiana, and claimed to be a relative. She had corresponded with Bill for some months and sent him her photograph. She wrote frequently after he was sentenced and at last her letters showed that she was greatly worried at receiving no replies, fearing she had written something to incur his displeasure. She finally wrote him a sad and last farewell, expressing the deepest sympathy and begging him, if he ever became free, to be certain to visit.

The day Cherokee Bill was told that his last chance for clemency was gone was an eventful day. He was given a new cell, his games of poker were ended, and no prisoner was allowed to come in front of his door or to converse with him. A guard was appointed to sit in front of his cell constantly. He was allowed a deck of cards with which to play "solitaire." He appeared to be in a fairly happy state of mind and talked freely about his upcoming execution, saying that the worst consideration was how his mother was going to take it. He paid much tribute to his attorney, J. W. Reed, who he said had worked with the same zeal as if he had been certain to receive a large fee. To the last, Cherokee Bill maintained his innocence of the majority of crimes charged to him, and even refused to admit that he killed Lawrence Keating. He said, "I don't know whether I killed him or not. I don't know whether my shots struck him. He may have been shot by the guard."

The *Fort Smith Elevator* newspaper wrote about Bill:

> *He is as reckless as and careless as ever . . . defiant as when the bars first closed behind him . . . passes all his time, playing solitaire . . . keeps the door of his cell covered with a cloth, which is raised only when no strangers are about. Whenever a visitor enters the jail corridors the cloth goes up, and only the promise of twenty-five cents will induce Bill to show himself.*

On February 17, 1896, U.S. Marshal George C. Crump received a letter from a kinetoscope company requesting permission to photograph Cherokee Bill's execution. The request was forwarded to Washington, D.C. where it was denied. President Cleveland's new attorney general, Judson Harmon, instructed Crump to make the execution private, no cameras allowed. There was great disappointment because Crump had promised to the citizenry that the hanging would be public.

As the execution date drew near Cherokee Bill received religious readings and advice from the Reverend Father Pius of the German Catholic Church in Fort Smith. On Monday morning, March 16, the day before his execution, his mother, his brother Clarence; and old Amanda Foster, who had nursed him in infancy, arrived at the jail. This was their first visit to Bill since his re-sentencing.

His brother, Clarence, was allowed a few moments with the prisoner. Cherokee told him, "If I could hear of Ike Rogers being dead, I would be better satisfied to die . . ."

His mother was allowed to talk to him for a few hours in his cell. Lawyer Reed was there and a will was drawn up, Cherokee Bill gave his mother his allotment he had claimed in the Cherokee Nation, six miles from Talala. Clarence decided to walk around the jail yard and visited the scaffold and saw the rope which was being tested by a heavy wooden dummy.

On the day of the execution Fort Smith was inundated with all types of people. An estimated 3,000 sightseers came by rail, wagon, horseback and afoot, wanting to see the noted outlaw swing. The streets around the jail were not disorderly but filled with extreme excitement. Despite Marshal Crump's order to keep the affair strictly private, with no tickets of admission except to the necessary officials, physicians, clergy, and reporters, hundreds were given passes and were standing around the front gate. A number of people stood on the stone walls, people were standing on the roofs of nearby buildings. Nearby home owners even sold window and roof space for viewing opportunities.

The *Fort Smith Elevator* newspaper gave the following account of Cherokee Bill's execution:

> *Cherokee Bill awakened this morning at six, singing and whistling. He partook of a light breakfast about eight o'clock, which was sent to him by his mother from the hotel. At 9:20, Cherokee Bill's mother and the old negress who raised him were admitted to his cell, and shortly after Father Pius, his spiritual advisor, was also admitted. The*

usual noise and hubbub that is always heard within the big iron cage that surrounds the cells were noticeably lacking this morning.

Cherokee Bill's fellow prisoners, many of them under sentence of death seemed to be impressed with the solemnity of the occasion, and an air of subdued quiet pervaded the jail. Many of the men are already standing within the shadow of the gallows gathered in a group near the cell occupied by the condemned man an conversed in low tones. To his most intimate associates since his confinement, Cherokee distributed his small effects. . . .

By 10:30. The corridor in front of Cherokee's cell was crowded with newspaper representatives, deputy marshals, and other privileged individuals, all taking note of every passing incident. Occasionally the condemned man would throw aside the curtain which concealed the interior of his cell and make appearance at the grated door in order to give some instructions or make some request of the officer who stood guard.

About eleven o'clock Marshal Crump, after a short conversation with Cherokee, announced that the execution would be postponed until two o'clock, in order to give his sister an opportunity to see him before the death sentence was carried out. She was coming in on the east-bound Valley train, and would not arrive until one o'clock. The 2,000 or 3,000 sight-seers surrounding the big stone wall and within the enclosure dispersed.

It was a struggling mass of humanity that had gathered on and around the steps and walls and when the time came there was a scramble even among those who were provided with passes. There was a crush and a jam for a

A drawing depicting Cherokee Bill's hanging with the image of Larry Keating in the foreground.

few minutes but order was at last restored in a measure and all awaited the moment when the door should open for the coming of the condemned man. On the inside there was a repetition of the scenes of the morning. Bill's mother had packed up several belongings of her son and was ready when called upon to take final leave. Her parting was an affectionate one but she strove as much as lay in her power to restrain her emotion.

Bill was affected by it, but following the example of his mother, gave little or no indication that he was other than perfectly composed.

"Well, I am ready to go now most anytime," said he addressing the guards.

He was taken at his word and the juil was cleared. The crowd outside had swelled to increased numbers, all the available buildings and sheds being occupied. A pathway was cleared through the crowd, and very shortly after the clock struck two the door opened and the doomed man was brought forth, a guard on either side. The march to the gallows was taken up, and at Col. Crump's suggestion, Cherokee's suggestion, Cherokee's mother and the old col- ored Aunty walked alongside Bill. Father Pius came next, the newspaper men following and the crowd bringing up the rear.

"This is about as good a day to die as any," remarked Cherokee as he glanced around. Arriving at the south end of the jail, he looked around at the crowd and said, "It looks like a regiment of soldiers."

He continued to look around at the crowd, eyeing them curiously.

At the door of the enclosure there was a jam. Every- body crowded up and there was a stop for a few minutes. It took several minutes for everyone holding tickets to gain admittance, and by this time the condemned man and guards had mounted the scaffold. Bill walked with a firm step and, taking up a position near the west wall of the gallows, waited for the end.

Turning slightly and seeing his mother standing near, he said, "Mother, you ought not have come here." Her re- ply was: "I can go wherever you go."

Colonel Crump suggested to him that he take a seat until all was in readiness, but he replied, "No, I don't want to sit down."

The death warrant was then read, during which Bill gazed about as if a little impatient to have the thing over with. He was asked at its conclusion if he had anything to day, and replied, "No Sir, without he (meaning Father Pius) wants to say a prayer."

The priest here offered a short prayer, the condemned man listened attentively the meanwhile, and then as if knowing what was to come next, he walked forward till he stood upon the trap. Deputy Lawson and others arranged the ropes, binding his arms and legs, and it was while this was being done that Bill spoke to different ones in the crowd below.

"Good-bye, all you chums down that way," said he, with a smile. Just then he caught sight of a young man in the act

The Fort Gibson commissary where Cherokee Bill's body lay in state following his execution.

of taking a snap shot with a Kodak and pulling it sharply back. There was a creaking sound as the trap was sprung and the body shot downward. The fall was scarcely six feet, but the rope had been adjusted carefully by Lawson and the neck was broken. The muscles twisted once or twice, but that was all . . . Twelve minutes from the time the trap was sprung, the ropes that bound his limbs were removed, also the handcuffs and shackles, and the body was lowered into a coffin and borne away and crowd dispersed. At Birnie's, the coffin was placed in a box and then taken to the Missouri Pacific depot and put aboard the train. His mother and sister took it back with them to Fort Gibson.

The reporter from the main newspaper in the Indian Territory, The *Muskogee Phoenix* also gave a description of the execution of Cherokee Bill:

Cherokee Bill Hanged
His Mother and Old Nurse Stood by Him on the Gallows – Nervy to the Last.

Fort Smith, Ark. March 17 – The old gallows, which has so often done duty for the government, today claimed its seventy-fifth victim in the person of Crawford Goldsby, alias Cherokee Bill.

Up to Thursday Bill had made no preparation to meet his doom, but spent much of his time each day playing poker with other prisoners, manipulating the cards through the grating of his cell door. On Thursday last he accepted religious advice from Rev. Father Pius, of the German Catholic Church, and from that on received instruction in that faith each day.

On Monday his mother, sister and brother arrived, and his mother was allowed to spend some time with her son. He made a will which was drawn up by his attorney, J. W. Reed, in which he gave his mother his farm in the Indian Territory.

He retired about 9 o'clock last night and apparently slept soundly, awakening this morning at 6, singing and whistling. He partook of a light breakfast about 8 o'clock, which was sent to him by his mother from the hotel.

At 9:20 o'clock Cherokee Bill's mother and the old negress who raised him were admitted to his cell, and shortly after Father Pius.

About 11 o'clock Marshal Crump announced that the execution would be postponed until 2 o'clock, in order to give his sister an opportunity to see him before the death sentence was carried out. Then the 2000 sightseers surrounding the big stone wall and within the enclosure dis-

persed, to reassemble at 2 o'clock, when the march to the gallows began.

Upon emerging from the cell door Cherokee Bill gave a searching glance at the big crowd that lined the wall and that stood within the jail yard and remarked, "My, look what a crowd of people."

His arms and feet were manacled. By his side walked his mother and the old negress who raised him. They accompanied him up the steps leading to the scaffold and remained until all was over.

Just before the black cap was placed over his head he kissed his mother good-bye. She showed no signs of emotion, but when the trap was sprung turned her back upon the scene.

When asked if he had anything to say, he replied. "No; I came out here to die, not to talk."

After stepping upon the trap he looked down upon the upturned faces and, seeing an acquaintance, said "Good-bye Scott; take care of Dollie."

The trap was sprung at 2:15 and in fifteen minutes the physician pronounced him dead. His neck was broken in the fall. His body was turned over to relatives and by them taken to Ft. Gibson for burial.

Cherokee Bill's Crime

The crime for which Crawford Goldsby, alias Cherokee Bill paid the penalty to-day with his life was committed at Lenapah, a small station on the Kansas and Arkansas Valley Railroad in the Cherokee Nation, about 145 miles west of Fort Smith, on the 8th day of November, 1894. The particulars have heretofore been published.

The Outlaw's History

The criminal career of Cherokee Bill was brief, but

bloody to the extreme. He was born at Fort Concho (now San Angelo), Texas, February 8, 1876, his father being a soldier in the regular army (10ᵗʰ Cavalry). His mother and father separated during his childhood, and at the age of 17 he was living with his mother at Fort Gibson. Up to this time he had been a law-abiding young man. In November, 1893, he had trouble with a Negro named Jake Lewis, the latter kicking Bill in the stomach. Bill swore he would have revenge, and nest morning laid for him and shot him two or three times, but not fatally. Jake is still living at Fort Gibson. Bill escaped after the shooting and went on the scout, going into the neighborhood of his father's residence. While dodging the officers he fell in with the Cook gang and took a hand in several daring robberies, and soon gained the reputation of being the worst man in the gang. Bill and Jim Cook and Cherokee Bill were at the house of Cook's sister, fourteen miles from Tahlequah. The authorities wanted the Cooks for alleged horse stealing and Deputy Sheriff Ellis Rattlingourd, with a posse of seven men, went out to arrest them. A fight ensued in which Sequoyah Houston, of the Sheriff's posse, was killed and Jim Cook was shot seven times, but escaped. After the fight Bill Cook and Cherokee Bill took Jim to the neighborhood of Ft. Gibson, where they pressed a doctor into service and had his wounds dressed, but the officers pressed them so hard that they finally had to abandon Jim and he fell into the hands of the Cherokee authorities and is now serving a sentence in the National Prison for the killing of Houston.

The killing, capturing and scattering of the Cook gang by the vigorous work of the authorities caused Cherokee Bill to scout alone for some time in the vicinity of Nowata, where his sister lived. Shortly before his arrest he killed his brother-in-law, Brown, with whom he quarreled. The mysterious killing of Agent Richards at Nowata was believed to be his work, and he is charged with killing a brakeman on a freight train near Ft. Gibson in June, 1894. His capture, and then his killing of Larry Keating, a guard, in the jail here, are fresh in the memory of our readers.

It was noteworthy that the same newspaper on April 2 again printed a reported quote of Cherokee Bill's at the execution:

Cherokee Bill's dying words were: "I came not here to talk but to die. Proceed with the killing business."

Cherokee Bill's family took his body to Fort Gibson where a wake and funeral were held in the old military commissary building. He was buried in the Cherokee National Cemetery in Fort Gibson later named the Citizens Cemetery of Fort Gibson not far from other companions Jim French and the Verdiris KId. Some of the most important citizens in Cherokee history in the Indian Territory are buried in this cemetery along with Cherokee Bill, his mother and siblings. A recent headstone in the 1990s was placed on their gravesite with incorrect dates for the children. It listed Cherokee Bill as the youngest.

After Cherokee Bill's execution, there was much talk concerning his relationship to the number thirteen. It was believed by some that he killed thirteen people during his outlaw career. The offer of $1300 reward affected his capture for killing Ernest Melton; his first sentence to die was pronounced on April 13; he killed Keating on the 26th day of July or twice thirteen; Bill was said to have fired thirteen shots, during the attempted jail break; Judge Parker occupied thirteen minutes in charging the jury in the Keating case; the foreman of the jury was boarded in house during the trial that had the house number of 313; the actual hours occupied in the trial, numbered thirteen; the jury were thirteen minutes in arriving at a verdict; the jurymen and deputy, who ate and slept together during the trial made a company of thirteen; his last thirteen steps were up to the platform of the gallows; there were thirteen witnesses for prosecution; he fell through the trap at 2:13 o'clock; and there were thirteen knots in the hangman's noose.

I am not certain Cherokee Bill killed thirteen people but those who are known to be murder victims of Cherokee Bill include the barber, J. M. Mitchell of Chandler; Cherokee lawman Sequoyah Houston; Missouri Pacific Railroad Conductor Sam Collins, when he insisted Cherokee Bill pay his fare or get off his train; Station agent Dick Richards, shot while resisting a hold-up; Ernest Melton, shot during the hold-up of the store in Lenapah; Mose Brown, his brother-in-law; and Lawrence Keating.

There may have been more killings but I haven't been able to account for them. All the robberies and thefts by Cherokee Bill will never be known. I was told that Ellen Lynch, Cherokee Bill's mother, kept a life size artistic drawing of Bill in the living room of her home for the rest of her life in Fort Gibson. There is no knowledge of what happened to the artwork.

Chapter Thirteen

Revenge

As reported earlier in the text, Ike Rogers and Cherokee Bill were friends, and with his capture Cherokee Bill felt he had been betrayed by one of his best friends in the Cherokee Nation. It was even reported that Cherokee Bill would hide out at Rogers' home until he could go forth in comparative safety at various times. Right before he was hanged, Cherokee Bill told his brother Clarence, "If I could hear of Ike Rogers being dead, I would be better satisfied to die . . . ." Clarence didn't forget the words of his brother.

Clarence had always been a quiet and well-mannered youth, and had the respect and confidence of all good citizens of Fort Gibson, his home. A certain animosity grew into his heart against Ike Rogers on account of the latter's betrayal of his brother, but was never manifested in any overt act. Then, in the town of Hayden, Cherokee Nation, in the winter of 1897, the paths of Clarence and Ike crossed, nearly a year after Cherokee Bill's execution.

At Hayden, for a month or more, were located the officials of the Indian Freedmen payment to the black citizens of the Cherokee Nation. These were individual shares in the money received by the United States government, from the sale of the Cherokee Strip. Clarence Goldsby was entitled to a portion of this money, on account of being the son of a black citizen, and was one of the thousands who traveled to Hayden to receive this money. There he met Ike Rogers, who was present for the same purpose.

Rogers had received earlier $1,200 for the capture of Cherokee Bill and was still proudly bragging about these exploits. Clarence confronted Rogers and quarreled with Rogers about the wrongs done to his brother. Rogers pulled a pistol on Clarence and held it to his head; he then proceeded to abuse him and call Clarence vile names and epithets. Later, Clarence was heard to tell some friends, "I'm going to kill that damn' Negro marshal."

William Lee Starr, a Cherokee Freedman, gave the following interview in the *Indian Pioneer Papers* of this encounter:

> . . . *I was at the Cherokee Freedmen payment at Hayden. On one of the dancing platforms Clarence and Ike began a dispute about something concerning the arrest of Cherokee Bill. Ike gave Clarence a shove and made some threat. The officials of the payment decided to move the payment to Fort Gibson. Clarence told Ike Rogers that if he put his foot on the soil at Fort Gibson he would be a dead man.*
>
> *But Ike was not to be bluffed. He notified Clarence that he would be down on the morning train which arrived in Fort Gibson about 10:30 a.m. and that he was ready for him. . . .*

Fort Gibson storekeeper Alex R. Matheson, interviewed for the *Indian Pioneer Papers* said:

> . . . *Clarence Goldsby, Cherokee Bill's brother went to Hayden to attend the payment. . . . Ike Rogers, a Negro U.S. marshal who was instrumental in getting Cherokee Bill caught was there. When Clarence got back he came in the store and told us how Rogers had abused him in every way imaginable. He broke down and cried like a baby, said*

*he was going to kill that damn Negro marshal. Sometime
later he found out in some way that Rogers was going to
be on the ten o'clock train the next night [morning]. I was
city clerk at that time. About four o'clock, Clarence came
to me and wanted a commission to carry a gun. I issued
him the commission. . . .*

The Cherokee Freedmen payment in Fort Gibson was actually about a month later after the payments in Hayden. The comments by Matheson, are interesting due to the fact that Ike Rogers was hired by the Cherokee Nation as a guard for the Freedmen payments. A city clerk is a political position; Fort Gibson was one of the major towns in the Cherokee Nation. We know from previous testimony that Rogers had been highly critical with U. S. government officials of the Cherokee Nation's treatment of their Indian Freedmen community. Could Cherokee Nation officials have wanted the possibility of Rogers being silenced, by taking advantage of the animosity and friction between him and Goldsby? Or, did City Clerk Matheson just want to give Clarence Goldsby a chance to defend himself by giving him a gun permit?

The *Muskogee Morning Times* on April 21, 1897 carried the following story:

IKE ROGERS KILLED.

Clarence Goldsby Commits Murder at Fort Gibson.
MADE HIS ESCAPE.
*A Bystander Shot in the Jaw --- Officers Scouring the
Country.*
Special to the Muskogee Morning Times.
Fort Gipson. April 20. (Copyright)
*---About 10 o'clock yesterday morning at Ft. Gibson,
Clarence Goldsby shot and killed Ike Rogers. Both men*

half-breeds.

Ike Rogers alighted from the eastbound train was in the act of shaking hands with friends standing standing on the depot platform when Clarence Goldsby drew his pistol and fired. The ball missed Rogers and lodged in the jaw of a bystander. Goldsby fired three more shots, each taking effect, two in the head and one in the body of Rogers. Rogers fell and expired immediately, Goldsby seized Rogers' Winchester and darted under the train standing alongside of the platform. By the time those in pursuit crossed the train the murderer had covered considerable ground. About forty shots were fired after the fugitive but failed to take serious effect if any.

Officers were at once notified and started in pursuit. Eight deputy marshals are on duty searching for the murderer.

It was reported last night that a posse surrounded Goldsby in a clump of bushes and could not rout him. They hitched their horses near the edge of the brush and began searching inside. After a diligent search the posse gave up the hunt only to find that in the meantime Goldsby had made his escape on one of the horses belonging to the posse.

Clarence is a brother of the famous Crawford Goldsby generally known as "Cherokee Bill." Crawford and Clarence were born near San Angelo, Texas, in 1876 and 1877 respectively. Their father and mother separated when they were small boys. The boys and their mother moved to Fort Gibson. . . .

. . . Ever since Ike Rogers planned and captured Cherokee Bill, it has been the opinion of many that Clarence Goldsby would get even with him.

During the freedmen payment at Hayden, Clarence Goldsby and Ike Rogers had some trouble and Clarence told Ike, "If you ever come to Fort Gibson, I will take your scalp." The Rogers folks at Fort Gibson sent Ike word to [not] come along. He went to Fort Gibson. When Ike Rogers arrived Clarence Goldsby met him at the depot with the results given above.

The *Muskogee Phoenix* newspaper on April 22, 1897 wrote:

Killing of Ike Rogers

Tuesday morning, at the arrival of the east bound Valley passenger train, about 10 o'clock, Clarence Goldsby shot and killed Ike Rogers on the depot platform at Fort Gibson. This tragedy is not in any way connected with the present payment, but is the outcome of violent deeds during other years.

Rogers was the man who effected Cherokee Bill's capture, which it will be remembered, was accomplished by betrayal of Bill's confidence. This has rankled the breasts of Cherokee Bill's kinsmen and friends, and Clarence Goldsby, a younger brother of Cherokee, declared he would kill Rogers. At the payment at Hayden, Rogers is said to have questioned young Goldsby about this threat, even presenting a gun at his head and otherwise abusing him. The youngster was at that time unarmed, but informed Rogers that if he ever came to Ft. Gibson the killing would certainly be done. So the matter rested until Tuesday morning. It is said the wife of Rogers telegraphed him not to go to Ft. Gibson but his confidence was supreme.

Tuesday morning Rogers alighted from the train and was in the act of shaking hands with Attorney Osborne, of Muskogee, when Goldsby advanced upon the back and right side of Rogers and shot through the neck with a large revolver. Rogers gave but a groan as he fell and Goldsby continued to advance and fire until five shots were fired. It is thought the first shot broke the man's neck, the bullet passing onward inflicting a very serious wound in the mouth and jaw of Tolly Elliott, porter at Hotel Trent. Two other bullets entered the prostrate body of Rogers, one in the cheek and the other in the right eye. Two shots missed. As Rogers fell his Winchester dropped from his right hand and was seized by Goldsby, who dodged under a passenger car, across the tracks and under a freight car and passed up one of the main streets of the town. A shower of bullets followed him from the pistols of several deputies; sometimes answered back by shots from Rogers' gun in Goldsby's hand. Probably the last shot fired was by Commissioner McCombs, who fired as he turned a corner. Deputy Bill Taylor and Policeman Ran Lee followed the fugitive until he was hemmed in a thicket and they were forced to dismount. They hoped for the arrival of reinforcements, but finally began reconnoitering without their horses. While this was going on, Goldsby stole a march on Policeman Lee, seized his horse, a good one, and was off at full speed. Pursuit was abandoned for a time, but is being systematically carried on at the present time.

Clarence Goldsby is but 19 years of age, unmarried, well known and liked in Ft. Gibson. He was very steady and quiet was often employed by firms in draying business and the like. Even now, with the blood of this man on his hands, kind words are spoken and sympathy for him are freely expressed.

Rogers gained his reputation by the capture of Cherokee Bill and it probably also added to his recklessness. Hav-

ing been an officer of the United States at one time, though he and Goldsby both belonged to the Cherokees, the case becomes one for the United States jurisdiction.

Rogers's wife was separated from him and running a lunch stand at the upper tent town. It is thought she warned him not to come partly for his own good and also to avoid his presence at the payment.

It is currently reported that Goldsby received four of five bullet holes in his clothing and that one bullet had given him a slight flesh wound in the right side.

A warrant is out for Goldsby, but at the very last information to be had his whereabouts is not known.

Another newspaper story concerning the incident at Fort Gibson was printed by the *Van Buren Press* of Arkansas, a town located next door to Fort Smith:

Cherokee Bill's Brother Takes Bloody Revenge
Special to the Post-Dispatch.
Fort Gibson, I.T., April 20. – Ike Rogers the man who captured Crawford Goldsby, alias Cherokee Bill, came in on the 10:30 train this morning and had hit the platform when he was shot by Clarence Goldsby, a brother of Cherokee Bill.

Rogers lived at Nowata, about seventy miles west of here, and knew that Cherokee Bill's brother was only waiting for an opportunity to kill him. Not less than 200 people were on the depot platform when the shooting occurred.

The first ball took effect in Rogers' body. Then the people crowded away and Goldsby fired three shots from a six-shooter into Rogers' head. Then he picked up Rogers' Winchester rifle, which had fallen between the platform and the railroad tracks, and ran under the car to the oth-

er side. There, about fifty shots were exchanged, only one stray bullet taking effect, it striking a colored man in the face, inflicting a painful but not necessarily fatal wound.

The Cherokee freedman's payment is going on here and not less than 5,000 people are camped here. It is a motley set of Negroes, Indians and whites, the Negroes predominating. Rogers was a Cherokee Negro and has been considered a peaceable citizen. Clarence Goldsby, who did the shooting is about 21 years old, and has always been considered a peaceable, inoffensive boy. Excitement is a little high yet, but no further danger is apprehended.

It was said that during the following month Clarence returned to Fort Gibson, under cover of darkness, two or three times, to his mother's house, when, acting on the advice of friends of the family, he left the Indian Territory. It was also said that after Clarence's initial run from the law there was never a concerted effort made for his capture.

We now know that after Clarence left Fort Gibson he went to St. Louis, Missouri. Clarence's death certificate from Missouri states that he was married and worked as a railroad Pullman porter in the gateway city. Clarence died of pneumonia at the age thirty-three on February 18, 1911. His body was shipped back to Fort Gibson where he was buried with his family in the cemetery.

Cherokee Bill's youngest brother, Luther died in April of 1912. The *Fort Gibson New Era* newspaper said that Luther had grown to over six feet tall and weighed 260 pounds. The newspaper said Luther was fine looking and a man of peace. It didn't give a reason for death in the May 2, 1912 newspaper.

Maud Brown Surrell, Cherokee Bill's niece in January

of 1938, in an interview for the *Indian Pioneer Papers* project said the following concerning her uncle's:

> *The fugitive career of my uncle Crawford Goldsby, known as Cherokee Bill, and his brother Clarence, of course, is in the Annals of Indian Territory history, but I believe if they could have had an opportunity, different environment and proper training during their younger life, they would have been different men.*

This did not end the outlawry in the Goldsby family lineage. Research shows that Cherokee Bill's sister Georgia had two children, a girl named Gertrude born around 1895 to Mose Brown, and a son named Marcus Trainor who was born around 1896. Some researchers have said that Gertrude was the daughter of lawyer J. Warren Reed, who defended Cherokee Bill.

Marcus was the son of the well known Cherokee desperado/outlaw Bud Trainor who was responsible for many misdeeds in the Indian Territory. Including the murder of Deputy U.S. Marshal Dan Maples for which Ned Christy was accused and lost his life. Marcus later took the married name of his mother of Foreman, and he was referred to sometimes as Mark Foreman.

On September 29, 1916, three black men attacked Sheriff James Mayes at the Nowata County jail in an attempted jail break. The leader of the outlaw crew was Mark Foreman who was under arrest for carrying a concealed pistol and illegal discharge of firearms. As they sat in jail, Foreman asked Sheriff Mayes for something to eat. Mayes sent a young boy to a restaurant to pick up enough food for the three prisoners. When the Sheriff opened the steel door to feed the prisoners, they rushed him knocking him down to the floor.

During the jail break, Deputy Sheriff James P. Gibson ran to assist the sheriff, Foreman got control of the sheriff's gun and shot Gibson fatally. Taking the dead deputy's pistol, Foreman and Sonny Powell then escaped from the jail. Foreman and Powell ran to a house on the edge of town and the other man went on his way. Instead of leaving town after the jail break, Foreman and Powell hung around town and robbed two other men, one of them a police officer whose weapon they took.

The location of their hiding place was well known to officers. Deputy Sheriff Wade Kivett put together a posse and surrounded the house. Kivett approached the front door as Foreman was standing on the other side gun in hand. Kivett kicked in the door and fired his weapon in the same instance hitting Foreman before he got a shot off. The fugitives surrendered immediately to the posse.

Foreman and Powell were arrested by law officers not more than three hours later after the jail break. A lynch mob formed of about 200 men took possession of the prisoners and attempted to lynch them in front of the Methodist Church down the street from the county court house. The Reverend Paul Pierce interceded, pleading with the mob to allow Foreman and Powell be tried in a court of law. The minister interjected that Foreman would probably die from his gunshot injury anyway, and letting the law take its course was the Christian thing to do. The mob was moved by the minister's words and turned the prisoners by over to Deputy Kivett and dispersed.

Around 8:30 p.m. that night a group of about seventy-five masked men stormed the jail, broke the steel doors open and Foreman and Powell were kidnapped. A noose was placed around Powell's neck, and he was dragged down the street to a nearby tree. The rope attached to Powell was thrown over the tree limb and he was hoisted in the air, where he was shot and hung simultaneously.

Next Foreman's hands were tied and a noose placed around his neck and he was hung from a nearby lamppost. Mark Foreman died at approximately the same age as his uncle Cherokee Bill, his execution illegal and Bill's legal, both for criminal misdeeds.

The saga of Cherokee Bill comes to a close, but the outlaw legend from eastern Oklahoma lives on. He was like a shooting star that shines real bright for a short period but then quickly flames out. If Jesse James, Butch Cassidy, Billy the Kid, and the Dalton's can be celebrated as American outlaws, there is no reason we cannot also celebrate the dashing firebrand Crawford Goldsby known as "Cherokee Bill." What is known is that Cherokee Bill's outlaw legacy remains forever in the annals of frontier Oklahoma history.

Chapter Fourteen

Cherokee Bill and the New York Times

I have read where some historians called Cherokee Bill a regional outlaw with no national following. I will post in this chapter some of the articles from the the the *New York Times* newspaper of New York City that followed Cherokee Bill and the Bill Cook Gang during their criminal career in the Indian Territory. The newspaper articles, from the largest city in the United States, show that Cherokee Bill did have a national following during his lifetime. The articles were written by correspondents based in the Indian Territory for the newspaper. The *New York Times* was one of the major urban newspapers in the late 19th century.

That Cherokee Bill was covered by this newspaper gave him more imminence than many Wild West characters of that era. In their articles sometimes they spell the town of Muskogee as Muscogee, the latter was the original way the town was spelled and later changed to the former. Most of the time, the newspapers in or closer to Indian Territory were more accurate with events and names than the *New York Times*. The articles are in chronological order.

October 24, 1894
AFTER THE "BILL" COOK GANG
A PITCHED BATTLE WITH THE OUTLAWS EXPECTED.
Posses of United States Marshals Pursuing them in the Indian Territory for Daring Robberies in Talala

and Watova and Other Outrages that Have Aroused the Settlers and the Indians – the Latter Appeal to the Government.

WAGONER, Indian Territory, Oct. 23. – Word reached this city at 8 o'clock tonight that "Bill" Cook and his band of desperadoes were encamped on Verdigris River, eight miles south of Wagoner. A posse of Marshals were hastily sworn in, and headed by Deputy United States Marshals Lawson and Hockbruner [Heck Bruner], left about 9:30 o'clock.

Hockbruner [Heck Bruner] has a national reputation as a brave man, and has done more to rid the Territory of desperadoes than any other Marshal in the Territory. He is the Marshal who blew up the house and killed the noted "Ned" Christy, who held the Government forces at bay for several days with a Gatling gun.

There is little doubt that the morning will brings news of an engagement between the Marshals and the bandits.

Talala, a station on the Kansas and Arkansas Valley Railroad, a branch of the Missouri Pacific system, forty-six miles west of Wagoner, was cleared out by the Cook band last night, and proceeded at once to rob stores left and right.

Every store in the place was visited and the proprietors compelled at the point of revolvers and rifles to turn over their cash.

The Post Office was robbed of stamps and a small amount of money.

While the bandits were in the Post Office the east-bound passenger train pulled in. The trainmen were soon notified of the gang's presence and the train started out at once. It is believed here that the gang intended to rob the train.

Neal Pryor of Fort Smith, who arrived here tonight, gives additional particulars. He said that the bandits, who numbered ten, made no effort to conceal their identity. They visited all of the stores, entering with drawn revolvers and compelling the frightened merchants to give up their money and valuables.

The bandits did not tarry long after the passenger train pulled out. They galloped out of town, discharging their rifles.

The robbing of the train at Corretta Saturday night by this notorious gang, which was followed by the delivery of "Jim" Cook, a brother of "Bill" Cook from the Tahlequah jail at Tahlequah yesterday, and the robbery of the station, Post Office, and only store at Watova, Indian Territory, and the Talala robberies, have awakened the authorities to the necessity of prompt action.

Indian Agent Wisdom of this city organized today his 100 United States Deputy Marshals in three posses. After meeting at Fort Gibson, Indian Territory, this afternoon, one posse was ordered southeast, to work their way north; one posse went directly east toward Tahlequah, and the other northeast, along Grand River.

The gang contemplates a raid on the Missouri, Kansas and Texas express train near Chetopa or Prior [Pryor] Creek, as they sent word that they would get even with the American Express Company for the killing of Rogers last year.

Part of the Cook gang went east through Fort Gibson this morning.

Chief Harris of the Cherokee Nation also has eighteen mounted Indian police on the trail of the Cook brothers.

October 25, 1894

MORE OUTRAGES BY "BILL" COOK'S GANG
Another town Robbed by the Outlaws —Marshals Hot After Them.

FORT SMITH, Ark., Oct. 24 – News was brought here to-day by Deputy United States Marshal that "Bill" Cook's gang of robbers, who have been robbing trains and looting towns in the Indian Territory, raided Gibson Station yesterday.

They looted all the shops, escaping with considerable booty, but it is not known exactly how much.

The band then raided the cotton fields in the vicinity and robbed the pickers at work. The authorities of the Indian Territory have offered a reward for the capture of the outlaws, who are being hotly pursued by Indian police and a strong posse of Deputy Marshals.

News of a fight in which the bandits may be exterminated, is looking for at any moment. The pursuing officers say they will show no quarter to the robbers.

October 28, 1894

REWARDS FOR THE COOK GANG.
For the Capture of the Outlaws $250 Apiece is Offered.

FORT SMITH, Ark., Oct. 27. – United States Marshal Crump of the Western District of Arkansas has had more than 5,000 posters scattered throughout this section, announcing a reward of $250 each for the bodies of the members of "Bill" Cook's gang of outlaws. The reward is authorized by the Attorney General of the United States, and is payable on approval of the court.

Deputy United States Marshals are debarred from participating in the reward, and this fact has stimulated large parties of settlers to join in the pursuit. The names of the outlaws for whom a reward is offered are:

"Bill" Cook, Crawford Crosby, alias "Cherokee Bill"; "Buck" Wightman, alias "Bitter Creek"; Columbus Means, "Skeeter" James French, Samuel Brown, Perry Brown, Thomas Quarles, "Joe" Jennings, Charles Clifton, George Newton, "Slaughter Kid," and "Bill" Doolin. Nothing had been heard at the Marshal's office to-day from the pursuing posse, which was last night in the vicinity of Sapulpa.

November 15, 1894

"BILL" COOK'S GANG AGAIN
Eluding All the Marshals and Police They Rob Another Train.
A Passenger Their Unwilling Assistant
Forced to Carry Through the Cars a Sack to Receive Others' Valuables
Agent Wisdom Again Ask for Troops.

WAGONER, Indian Territory, Nov. 14. – Notwithstanding the large force of United States Marshals and Indian police that has been surrounding the Cook gang of outlaws and pressing them hard, the gang broke through the armed circle of the law last night and stopped and robbed a Missouri, Kansas and Texas Railroad Train at Wybark, a blind siding, eleven miles south of Wagoner.

The scene, as described by a passenger apart from the anxiety and danger incident to the robbery, was amusing. As the train was being side-tracked the engineer and fireman, seeing the bandits, stopped the train and took to the woods, so that the robbers were unable to use them in forcing the messenger to open the express car.

The gang proceeded to place dynamite on the trucks of the express and baggage cars. Five sticks of dynamite were exploded, but only resulted in blowing holes in the bottoms of the cars.

One of the gang then entered the smoking car, while three on each side of it kept up a fusillade of bullets through the car. The robber who entered called for a volunteer to hold the sack, and, leveling his gun on a young man from Indiana, seated near the front of the car, said with an oath:

"You better throw your wad into this sack; then take the sack and pass it along, and if you don't do it quick I'll kill you."

The young man begged for mercy crying that he would do anything if the robber would not shoot. The robber, with the young Hoosier in advance, passed down the car, everybody but the women contributing liberally. The robber was not satisfied, however, shouting that not enough watches were coming in, and turned over the cushions of every seat, where he found many hidden watches.

Having passed through all the cars, the sleeper included, with a farewell volley the robbers left, taking the young Hoosier with them.

A few minutes later the passenger returned stating that the robbers had taken him a quarter of a mile and then turned him loose. It was a hard matter to find the engineer and fireman ever after the robbers had gone, as they were afraid of a sudden return of the gang. The train was delayed an hour.

All the windows were shot out and the sides of the cars were riddled with bullets. Seven men were engaged in the robbery, and they were undoubtedly led by "Bill" Cook, "Cherokee Bill," and "Dynamite Dick."

The robber who passed through the car is described as being a large, portly man, with ruddy complexion, blue eyes, and light hair, and wearing a false chin beard, but no mask. The robbers when leaving struck out for the bottoms between the Verdigris and Arkansas Rivers.

A posse from Muskogee and the surrounding country started in pursuit, but no tidings have so far been received.

November 17, 1894

"BILL" COOK'S GANG NOT AFRAID

The Bandits Ride Into Muskogee After a Fresh Supply of Cigars – Olney Demands Their Arrest.

MUSKOGEE, Indian Territory, Nov. 16. – "Bill" Cook's gang of outlaws seems to be fearless of capture. Yesterday the outlaws camp was discovered in the Arkansas bottoms, and United States Commissioner Jackson authorized a party of farmers and Deputy Marshals to effect their capture. They were to start at nightfall, but did not get away on schedule time.

Even while they were making their preparations for a fight to the death, the enemy was daring them to do their worst.

At about 10 o'clock last night twelve members of the gang rode into town. They paraded the main street, laid in a fresh supply of cigars, and then rode leisurely out of town.

Not a Deputy Marshal, Indian policeman, or bloodthirsty farmer was in sight during their stay. The posse declared after their departure that they could not get ready for the attack in time to give them battle, and so decided that it would be better to follow them.

Half an hour after the Cook gang had gone, the posse got in line. There were fifteen Marshals in a covered wagon, and a lot of Indian policemen, ten of whom were well mounted. They started out on the trail, declaring that they would capture the bandits.

The citizens of Muskogee and the Chiefs of the Creek and Cherokee Nations have become thoroughly disgusted with the Deputy Marshals and Indian police and have concluded to offer a reward sufficient to justify officers in coming from the States to capture the fifteen members of the Cook gang.

Fifteen hundred dollars has been offered for the capture of "Bill" Cook, Cherokee Bill, James French, Skeeter, and James Turner. The $500 reward offered by the United States Government and the $250 offered by Chief Harris of the Cherokee Nation failed to improve the courage of the Deputy Marshals and the Indian police.

Warrants for the arrest of "Bill" Cook, Cherokee

Bill, James French, James Turner, Skeeter, and "Bill" McElijah were placed in the hands of the Muskogee deputies Oct. 24, but no attempt has been made to arrest any of the gang.

Attorney General Olney has telegraphed the court officials of this place that lawlessness must be put down. Mr. Olney says he cannot understand why the Cook gang has not been captured, as the Territory has more Marshals and peace officers than many of the States.

This afternoon the Creek Light Horsemen came upon the fifteen Marshals and police about three miles west of Muskogee, and thinking the Marshals wee the bandits, surrounded them. The Marshals took the light horsemen for the bandits and prepared for the battle. The two posses of officers guarded each other for several hours, but only one shot was fired.

Chief Perryman of the Creek Nation received word of the situation, and he and the United States Attorney had to drive out to the ground to inform the two forces.

An Indian officer has just arrived and reported that the Cooks are not ten miles from Muskogee, and he is trying to get up a posse of officers to go after them.

It is well known that the robbers have been within ten miles of Muskogee for more than a week. The people have no protection. There is not a night in the week three or four members of the gang are not seen in the dives of this town.

November 18, 1894

CHEROKEE BILL IS WOUNDED
TWO OTHER MEMBERS OF THE GANG HAVE BEEN CAPTURED.

The Remainder of the Outlaw Band Surrounded - An Autograph Letter from Bill Cook.

Muskogee, Indian Territory, Nov. 17. – A telegram received by United States Attorney Jackson to-night states that Deputy Marshals had a fight this afternoon with Cherokee Bill and his gang. Cherokee Bill was badly wounded, and two other members of the party were captured, together with two of the bandits' horses. The deputies of the Fort Smith and Muskogee courts are hunting Cherokee Bill and the remaining members of the gang.

Marshal Rent Cobb arrived late to-day, bringing in one of the captured robbers and a whiskey peddler. The other members of the Cook gang are said to be surrounded by the Marshals. Cobb has asked the United States Attorney and the United States Marshal for recruits to assist him.

Cherokee Bill is so badly wounded that the deputies think he will soon be obliged to give himself up. Cobb reports that he expects a hard battle, but that he has the advantage of the bandits.

Excitement is running high in Muskogee, and a company of men is being organized to start to the scene of the battle.

Marshal McAlester is tired of being criticized, and has concluded to take some action. Out of twenty Marshals, McAlester can get only eight to pursue the bandits. A number of citizens have offered to assist in capturing the Cooks if their expenses are paid.

At a secret meeting of business men held early this morning, $1,000 was subscribed for the defense of the town. Ex-Indian Agent Leo E. Bennett was placed in command. He immediately held a conference with Al McKay, one of the Indian police, and a plan of campaign was perfected.

The town is to be guarded by armed men both day and night. Scouts are to be placed in the suburbs to watch the movements of "Bill" Cook and his men. All suspicious persons found in the town are to be arrested on sight. If any person resists arrest, he is to be shot down. The streets are filled with armed guards, and this show of force has evidently impressed the outlaws. The first suspicious character who attempts to enter the bank will be shot before he crosses the threshold.

"Bill ," Cook evidently does not fancy the charged situation. This morning he sent a letter to Attorney Jackson. It is written in his own handwriting, and on a single sheet of note paper, and is addressed to the Prosecuting Attorney. The following is a copy:

Camp Cook. –We found out to-day that you fixed up some Deputy Marshals to run us down. I mean me and my gang. If you are going to run us down, we will get you out of the way. We know what you do. If you let us alone, you are all right. If you don't, you will hear from us. Take Warning.

BILL COOK.

Among the marked men are Prosecuting Attorney Clifford L. Jackson, Leo E. Bennett, ex-Indian Agent; D. M. Wisdom, and United States Commissioner Wayman C. Jackson.

November 23, 1894

BILL COOK PROBABLY CAPTURED
A Posse After Three Members of the Gang – Muscogee Expects a Fight.

FORT WORTH, Texas, Nov. 22. – At the United States Marshal's office, though the officials are very reticent, it is regarded as positive that "Bill" Cook, the daring young leader of the gang which has been terrorizing the Indian Territory for the past five months, is under arrest. He is thought to be one of the five men captured by the Texas Rangers at Wichita Falls. The description of the man Farris exactly corresponds with that of "Bill" Cook. This is strengthened by the fact that the man who answers to the name of "Skeeter" is an exact counterpart of the man Baldwin, *alias* "Skeeter," of the Cook gang.

MUSCOGEE, Indian Territory, Nov. 22. – A courier who arrived in Muscogee at 1 o'clock this afternoon reports that three of the bandits, French, "Cherokee Bill," and "Lucky," are in the bottoms five miles north of here. A posse of fifteen men left for the bandits quarters at once. As the officers have been severely criticized by the citizens, it is believed that they will make a genuine effort to capture the bandits. The gang is headed in the direction of Muscogee. The citizens are preparing for a battle if the bandits attempt a raid. The bank is heavily guarded.

November 27, 1894
FIRED AT A FREIGHT TRAIN
The Engineer Kept on, Despite the Bandits
-Five of the Bill Cook Gang in Irons at Fort Smith.
FORT SMITH, Ark., Nov. 26. –Indian Agent Wisdom and ex-Indian Agent Bennett, both of Muscogee, have arrived from the bandit-infested part of the Territory. At Wagoner they were notified that the freight train just ahead of them had been fired into near Bragg station, whick is thirty miles east of Wagoner. Investigations proved the report true.

Seven men, mounted on horses and armed to the teeth, undertook to hold up the train in broad daylight, but the engineer and fireman lay down in the cab and let the train go ahead. A volley of bullets was fired at the cab, and as the caboose went by that was also fired into and riddled with bullets. The bandits sat on their horses, four on one side of the track and three on the other.

FORT WORTH, Texas, Nov. 26. –The "Skeeter" Baldwin quintet of the Cook gang, arrested by Texas Rangers at Bellevue, on the Fort Worth and Denver Road, ten days ago, were brought down from Wichita Falls last evening and taken to Fort Smith, where they will be tried. They were handcuffed, chained, well guarded by Deputy United States Marshals.

December 16, 1894
THE TERRITORY'S BANDITS
Why Officers of the Law Find Their Capture So Difficult.
PROTECTED BY A SECRET GUILD
They Have Friends Among the Indians, the Farmers, and

the Railroad.
Men Upon Whom Aid They Can Rely.

MUSCOGEE, Indian Territory, Dec. 16., -Only in the United States can be found a nation within a nation, and that nation practically without government. Here the strong man is the law, and the Anarchist finds his Elysium, if he can find happiness in a land where the weak are subject to the strong, where individual will is supreme, where property may be accumulated by one and taken possession by another.

Being the home of such outlaws as the Daltons, the Cooks, the Bills , with such prefixes as '"Cherokee," "Grasshopper," "Wild," and other equally expressive appellations, the world has come to believe that the little gang of outlaws are the real rulers and that the citizens are terrorized by their presence. The frequent train robberies in which these men figure conspicuously are supposed to be the work of desperadoes who are speedily hunted down, some killed, some captured, and the bands broken up. . . .

When the Dalton's invaded Coffeyville and the leader and several of his followers were killed and another wounded and captured, it was believed that order had been restored and lawlessness forever put down. Only a few weeks however, and Cook appeared upon the scene, trains were held up, stores robbed, and all the deviltry of the past was repeated and continued in spite of all the efforts of the United States Marshals and Indian police, supposed to outnumber the desperadoes fifty to one. . . .

. . . The Indians are their friends; those inclined to lawlessness are their friends; the farmers are their friends, and they have friends among the railroad men. They feel as secure in their calling as do the men who stand behind the counters in the great cities. They have their freedom, which means license to gratify all their evil passions. And this condition will exist as long as there is a nation within a nation, and that nation practically without government.

February 7, 1895

Train Robbers Convicted.

FORT SMITH, Ark., Feb. 6. – The jury in the Bill Cook and Cherokee Bill cases retired this afternoon and returned a verdict of guilty in twenty minutes. The convictions are for robbing the Wells-Fargo Express Company and the St. Louis and San Francisco Railroad Company at Red Fork, Indian Territory, July 18 last. There are several other cases against them.

April 24, 1895

"Bill" Cook on the Way to Albany.

FORT SMITH, Ark., April 23. – "Bill" Cook to-day began his journey to Albany, N.Y., where he will serve forty-five years in the penitentiary. He was taken in the special prison car, which is lined with sheet iron. The windows are heavily barricaded. In the special coach were nineteen other prisoners for the penitentiary at Albany.

Among them were Enoch Thomas and James and Edward Keeton, each of whom got ten years for manslaughter; Henry Buffington, a cousin of "Cherokee Bill"; Thomas Mowell, who with "Jim" French and John H. Beck, a Cherokee attorney, was convicted of making fraudulent certificates of Cherokee citizenship just before the payments last year. The others were cattle and horse thieves and whiskey peddlers.

July 28, 1895

Fort Smith, Ark., July 27. – In an attempt to liberate the prisoners in the United States jail yesterday, "Cherokee Bill," the outlaw shot and killed "Larry" Keating, the oldest guard on the force. "Cherokee Bill" is thought to have obtained the pistol from his sister. The outlaw did not get out of his cell.

August 13, 1895

"Cherokee Bill" to be Hanged Sept. 10

FORT SMITH, Ark., Aug. 12. –"Cherokee Bill" was sentenced this morning by Judge Parker to be hanged Sept. 10. Three weeks later, from the same scaffold, Mrs. Klittenring, George Washington, Richard Calhoun, John Allison, Elli Lucas, and Frank Carver are to be hanged simultaneously, all for murder.

September 19, 1895

UNDER TWO SENTENCES TO DEATH
Two Appeals Before the Supreme Court in Behalf of "Cherokee Bill."

WASHINGTON, Sept. 18. – For the first time in its history the Supreme Court of the United States now has pending before it two appeals by one person from judgments sentencing him to be hanged for murder, the two crimes having been committed on different days and at places separated by many miles. The appellant who presents this unique record is not yet twenty-one years of age.

"Cherokee Bill" was convicted Feb. 27 last in the court of Judge Isaac C. Parker, for the Western District of Arkansas, of the murder of Ernest Melton, in the Cherokee Nation, Indian Territory, Nov. 18, 1894, and sentenced to be hanged June 25, 1895. This murder, from the record, was committed out of pure wantonness. "Cherokee" and a companion, in broad daylight, rode up to the store of John Shufeldt, in Lenapah, and robbed the cash drawer and safe. As they were leaving the building "Cherokee" saw Melton watching them from a window in an adjoining house and shot him through the head, instantly killing him.

From the judgment in the case for that murder and appeal was taken by "Cherokee's" attorney, which reached the Supreme Court of the United States May 20, 1895. In the meantime he was confined in the jail at Fort Smith pending action upon the appeal. July 26 he shot and killed Lawrence Keating, a guard in the jail, two revolvers having been smuggled into the buildings by the prisoners. Saturday, Aug. 10, he was convicted of the second murder; two days later Judge Parker sentenced him to be hanged Sept. 10. The execution of this sentence was stayed by the filing of the appeal, and "Cherokee Bill" is still in jail.

November 24, 1895
MORE TROUBLE FOR "CHEROKEE BILL"
Although Under two Death Sentences
He Will Be Tried for Robbery.
FORT SMITH, Ark., Nov. 23. – Although twice convicted of murder, "Cherokee Bill" must stand trial for two of the robberies he committed in the Indian Territory.

New indictments were returned yesterday, and

were found, evidently, for the purpose of securing more rewards for the men who risked their lives for the capture of the young desperado.

The first indictment is for the train robbery at Red Fork, Indian Territory. The second is for robbing the Post Office at Lenapah, Nov. 9, 1894. "Cherokee Bill" and "Verdigris Kid" were the robbers in this. "Cherokee Bill" killed Ernest Melton, for which he was sentenced to be hanged before he killed Jail Guard Larry Keeling [Keating].

New indictments were also returned against "Nath" Reed, "Buse" Lucky, "Jim" Dyer, "Tom" Root, and "Will" Smith, for trying to rob the express car during the Blackstone affair.

December 3, 1895

CHEROKEE BILL TO BE HANGED
The Supreme Court Decides the Fate of the Outlaw
WASHINGTON, Dec. 2. – Crawford Goldsby, alias "Cherokee Bill," will have to hang for the murder of Ernest Melton in the Cherokee Nation, Nov. 18, 1894.

While engaged in robbing a store at Lenapah, Cherokee Bill shot and killed Melton. The Supreme Court to-day, in an opinion read by Justice White, affirmed the judgment in the Melton case, and "Cherokee Bill" will hang as soon as Judge Parker gets the mandate from the Supreme court.

March 15, 1896

"CHEROKEE BILL" MUST HANG.
WASHINGTON, March 14. – Crawford Goldsby, otherwise "Cherokee Bill," the most notorious Indian Territory outlaw, must hand on Tuesday next.

President Cleveland to-day denied Goldsby's application for clemency. " I have examined this application fully," he says, "and find no sufficient reason for commuting the sentence of the court or denying its execution. The Clerk of Pardons – will immediately notify the officers at Fort Smith that the judgment of the court must be carried out."

March 18, 1896

CHEROKEE BILL DIES SMILING.
Hanged at Fort Smith, Ark., While His Mother Stands by His Side.

FORT SMITH, Ark., March 17. – At 2:15 P.M. to-day Crawford Goldsy, alias Cherokee Bill was hanged. He was declared dead in ten minutes. The desperado showed no fear, and went to the trap the coolest man in the party. The execution was set for noon, but was postponed to allow the doomed man's sister to arrive here from Tahlequah.

On the gallows in reply to the question if he had anything to say he answered: "No, I came here to die, not to talk." Turning he kissed his mother good bye, and with a smile on his face walked to his place on the trap. Father Pius said a prayer while the doomed man was pinioned. Bill recognized friends inside the inclosure[sic], and calling them by name bade them good bye. Bill was smiling when the cap was drawn over his head. The noose was adjusted, and at 2:13 Turnkey Eoff sprang the lever and threw the trap.

Bill got his wonderful nerve from his mother. She stood by him on the gallows without flinching or shedding a tear. She took the body to Fort Gibson at

3 o'clock.

Crawford Goldsby was the name conferred upon Cherokee Bill when he was born at Fort Gibson, Indian Territory, Feb. 8, 1876. He was one of the few robbers who infested the Indian Territory during the reign of terror in 1894, and belonged to the Cook gang. He worked with Bill Cook on the ranch in the Creek Nation near Tulsa.

Cherokee Bill became an outlaw at the age of fourteen. He shot a man with whom he had quarreled, and from that time until his arrest he was on the scout, suspicious of every one except his mother and sister, and counting no friends so dear as his trusty rifle.

Bill's last robbery was the one which cost him his life. On Nov. 9 he and Verdigris Kid were robbing Lenapah when Ernest Melton looked out of his window to see what was the excitement outside. Bill saw him and sent a bullet through his brain. For this he was convicted on Feb. 27, 1895, and on April 15 was sentenced to be hanged on June 25. The sentence was stayed by an appeal to the Supreme Court, but the judgment of the lower court was confirmed, and he was again sentenced on Jan. 24, 1896.

One of the many murders charged to Bill was that of Agent Richards of Nowata. Bill strenuously denied this charge.

On the afternoon of July 26 Cherokee Bill put all Fort Smith in an uproar. He had secured a pistol, and coming out of his cell as the prisoners were being locked in he shot and killed Larry Keating. He also fired several shots at Turnkey Eoff, and kept up a fusillade with the guards for half an hour. It was a bold plot of the prisoner to break jail, but it failed.

[Author's note: Cherokee Bill was born in Fort Concho, Texas]

April 27, 1897

"CHEROKEE BILL" AVENGED.
Desperado's Brother Kills His Captor and Fires into a Crowd at Port [Fort] Gibson. I.T.

Port [Fort] Gibson, Indian Territory, April 21. – "Ike" Rogers the man who captured Crawford Goldsby, alias "Cherokee Bill." Came in on the 10:30 A. M. train yesterday, and had only set foot on the platform when he was shot by Clarence Goldsby, a brother of the desperado.

The first ball took effect in Roger's body. Then the people crowded away, and Goldsby fired three shots from a six-shooter into Roger's head. He then picked up Roger's Winchester rifle and ran under the car to the other side. There were fifty shots exchanged between him and the crowd. One ball struck a colored man in the face and inflicted a painful but not fatal wound.

The Cherokee freedmen's payment is going on here, and not less than 5,000 people are camped here. Rogers was a Cherokee Negro, and has been considered a peaceful citizen. Clarence Goldsby, who did the shooting is about twenty-one years old, and has always been considered a peaceful, inoffensive boy.

Bibliography

Documents

Cherokee Bill's Affidavit, March 16, 1896.

Crawford Goldsby, alias Cherokee Bill, Plaintiff in Error, vs. United States, No. 728, May 18, 1896; 16 U.S. 688; 16 Supreme Court Reporter 1201.

Grand Jury Report to the Hon. Isaac C. Parker, District Court of the Western District of Arkansas, August term, 1894, October 24, 1894.

Letter from Bill Cook (Autobiographical Sketch written in the U.S. Jail at Fort Smith, Arkansas, March 16, 1895).

Supreme Court of the United States, Crawford Goldsby, alias Cherokee Bill, Plaintiff in Error, vs. United States, No. 620, MANDATE, December 2, 1895.

United States vs. Crawford Goldsby, No. 1586, U.S. Commissioners Court, Fort Smith, Arkansas, filed March 7, 1894.

United States vs. Crawford Goldsby, alias Cherokee Bill, No. 106, U.S. District Court, Fort Smith, Arkansas, filed February 8, 1895.

United States vs. Crawford Goldsby, alias Cherokee Bill, and three others, No. 5050 (Grand Jury indictment – Robbery), U.S. District Court, Fort Smith, Arkansas, filed February 14, 1895; trial case No. 307.

United States vs. Crawford Goldsby, alias Cherokee Bill, and two others, No. 5057 (Grand Jury indictment – Robbery), U.S. District Court, Fort Smith, Arkansas, filed February 15, 1895; trial case No. 307.

United States vs. Crawford Goldsby, alias Cherokee Bill, No. 106 (Grand Jury Indictment – Murder), U.S. District Court, Fort Smith, Arkansas, filed February 14, 1895.

United States vs. Crawford Goldsby, alias, Cherokee Bill, No. 106 (Petition for Writ of Error), U.S. District Court, Fort Smith, Arkansas, filed May 4, 1895.

United States vs. Crawford Goldsby, alias Cherokee Bill, No. 132 (Motion in Arrest of Judgment), U.S. District Court, Fort Smith, Arkansas, filed August 3, 1895.

United States vs. Crawford Goldsby, alias Cherokee Bill, No. 132 (Grand Jury Indictment), U.S. District Court, Fort Smith, Arkansas, filed August 5, 1895.

United States vs. Crawford Goldsby, alias Cherokee Bill, No. 132 (Motion of continuance), U.S. District Court, Fort Smith, Arkansas, filed August 8, 1895.

United States vs. Crawford Goldsby, alias Cherokee Bill, No. 132 (Demurrer), U.S. District Court, Fort Smith, Arkansas, filed August 10, 1895.

United States vs. Crawford Goldsby, alias Cherokee Bill, No. 132 (Testimony and Proceedings), U.S. District Court, Fort Smith, Arkansas, filed August 10-12, 1895.

United States vs. Crawford Goldsby, alias Cherokee Bill, No. 132 (Bill of Exceptions), U.S. District Court, Fort Smith, Arkansas, filed August 12, 1895.

United States vs. Crawford Goldsby, alias Cherokee Bill, No. 132 (Motion for New Trial and Bill of Exceptions), U.S. District Court, Fort Smith, Arkansas, filed August 12, 1895.

United States vs. Crawford Goldsby, alias Cherokee Bill, No. 132 (Assignment of Errors), U.S. District Court, Fort Smith, Arkansas, filed August 24, 1895.

United States vs. Crawford Goldsby, alias Cherokee Bill, No. 5869 (Grand Jury indictment – Larceny of Money of U.S.), U.S. District Court, Fort Smith, filed November 22, 1895.

United States vs. Crawford Goldsby, alias Cherokee Bill, No. 176 (Sentence for Murder), U.S. District Court, Fort Smith, Arkansas, filed January 14, 1896.

George Goldsby, U.S. Bureau of Pensions, Depositions, Muskogee, Oklahoma, No. 1, 397, 777, Section 1.

Ellen Lynch, Notice of Special Examinations, Claim No. 1192048, U.S. Bureau of Pensions, Joplin, Missouri. June 14, 1923. Interview at Fort Gibson, Oklahoma.

Effie A. Scott, Claim No. 1198964, Docket F. 3144, U.S. Bureau of Pensions. Case Rejected on Appeal, January 24, 1924. Washington, D.C.

Newspapers

Afton News
Ardmore State Herald
Beaver County Democrat
The Chandler News
Claremore Progress
Daily Oklahoman
Dallas News
Edmond *Sun-Democrat*
Eufaula *Indian Journal*
Fort Smith News-Record
Fort Smith Elevator
Galveston Daily News
Guthrie Daily Leader
Kansas City Times
Muskogee Morning Times
Muskogee Phoenix
Muskogee Times Democrat
Northwest Arkansas Times
Oklahoma Daily Press-Gazette
Oklahoma Daily Star
Oklahoma Daily Times-Journal
Oklahoma State Capital
St. Louis Post Dispatch
South McAlester Capital
Stillwater *Eagle-Gazette*
Tahlequah Arrow
Tahlequah *Cherokee Advocate*
The New York Times
Vinita Indian Chieftain
Wichita Daily Eagle

Articles

Braun, Bill. "The Life and Hard Times of Crawford Goldsby." *True Frontier*, October 1974.

Breihan, Carl W. "Cherokee Bill Goldsby." *Real West*, January 1970; reprinted in *Old Timers Wild West*, December 1978.

Bristow, George, as told to Olevia E. Myers. "I Helped Capture Cherokee Bill!" *Frontier Times*, June-July 1967.

Burkholder, Edwin V. "The Tragic Weakness of Cherokee Bill." *Male*, July 1958.

"Cherokee Bill." *Gunslingers of the West*, Winter 1966-67.

Cotton, Robert, " 'Cherokee Bill' Was Among Most Bloodthirsty Outlaws." *Nowata Daily Star*, October 12, 1960.

Etter, Jim. "Cherokee Bill's Brother." *True West*, September-October 1974.

Etter, Jim. "The Day Sequoyah Houston Fell to Cherokee Bill." *Frontier Times*, October-November 1972.

Gordon, Wes. " 'Why Should I Use Fists to Fight? Guns is Better': Cherokee Bill." *Mens's Western*, August-September 1959.

Havelock-Bailie, Captain R. "Cherokee Bill's Last Stand." *True West Adventures*, Spring 1958.

Lehman, M.P. "A Good Day for Dying." *Golden West*, May 1965; reprinted in *The West*, February 1972.

"Life Record of Cherokee Bill." *Fort Smith Municipal Police Journal (annual)*, 1952.

McKennon, C.H. "The Scourge of the Territory." *Wildcat*, June 8, 1979.

McRae. Bennie J. "Crawford 'Cherokee Bill' Goldsby: The Toughest of Them All." *Lest We Forget (LWF) Publishing*, 1994.

Monan, Charles. "Unlucky 13." *Real West*, July 1960.

Penot, Barbara Hale. "The Hanging of Cherokee Bill." *True Frontier*, January 1969. Reprinted In *True Frontier*, Special Issue 1, 1971.

Smith, Nicka. "Finding Issac Rogers – Civil War Veteran, U.S. Deputy Marshal, Relatives." February 22, 2013. Internet: whoisnickasmith.com / genealogy

Stansbery, Lon R. "Cowtown Catoosa, 'Dark and Bloody Ground,' I.T." *Tulsa World*, July 27, 1937.

Stone, Arnold. "I Came to Die." *Real Adventure*, March 1957.

Turpin, Robert F. "Saga of the Deadly Cook Gang." *True Frontier*, November 1969; reprinted in *Best of the Badmen*, Sparta, Illinois: Majors Magazines, Inc., 1973.

Whitmire, Mrs. E.H. "A short Sketch of the Life of Cherokee Bill." Indian-Pioneer History, Oklahoma Historical Society, Archives and Manuscript Division, Vol. 11, 378-82.

Wing, Tom. "Cherokee Bill & Ike Rogers," *Do South Magazine*. February 1, 2018, internet: Dosouthmagazine.com

Winston, Morris, "A Murderer is Loose on the Cherokee Strip." *Great West*, April 1967.

Interviews

In *Indian-Pioneer History*, Oklahoma Historical Society, Archives and Manuscripts Division, Volumes 1 -112.

Byrd, William. Vol. 1, 482.

Calhoun, James Vol. 18, 128-29.

Griffin, Frank I. Vol. 26, 439-40.

Hill, Fielden Salyer. Vol. 29, 129.

Humberd, John C. Vol. 5, 287.

McDermott, Jess. Vol. 7, 14-15.

Matheson, Alex R. Vol. 6, 435-36.

Reynolds, John M. Vol. 41, 378-79.

Ross, Elizabeth. Vol. 42, 489-90.

Scott, J.W. Vol. 44, 19-20.

Still, Amanda L. Vol. 10, 164.

Surrell, Maude Brown. Vol. 87, 483-84.

Taylor, Burl. Vol. 10, 315-16, 320.

Taylor, William. Vol. 10, 349-52.

Turley, James W. Vol. 11, 51-53.

Warren, Clarence O. Vol. 11, 228-29, 232-33.

Books

Burton, Art T. Black, *Red and Deadly: Black and Indian Gunfighters of the Indian Territory, 1870-1907*. Austin, Texas, Eakin Press, 1991. Published currently by Wild Horse Media, Fort Worth, Texas.

Burton, Art T. *Black, Buckskin and Blue: African American Scouts and Soldiers on the Western Frontier*. Austin, Texas, Eakin Press, 1999. Published currently by Wild Horse Media, Fort Worth, Texas.

Burton, Art T. *The Real Cherokee Bill: Oklahoma Outlaw*. Self Published, 2003.

Conley, Robert J. *The Cherokee Nation: A History*. Albuquerque: University of New Mexico Press, 2005.

Clark, Charles N. *Lynchings in Oklahoma: A Study of Vigilantism, 1830-1930*. Self Published, 2000.

Conley, Robert J. *A Cherokee Encyclopedia*. Albuquerque: University of New Mexico Press, 2007.

Conley, Robert J. *The Witch of the Goingsnake and other Stories*. Norman, Oklahoma: University of Oklahoma Press, 1988.

Conley, Robert J. *Cherokee*. Graphic Arts Center Publishing, 1988.

Croy, Homer. *He Hanged Them High*. New York: Duell, Sloan and Pearce; Boston: Little, Brown and Company, 1952,

Drago, Harry Sinclair. *Outlaws on Horseback*. New York: Dodd, Mead and Company, 1964.

Emery, J. Gladstone. *Court of the Damned*. New York: Comet Press Books, 1959.

Gideon, D.C. *Indian Territory: Descriptive, Bibliographical and Genealogical…With a General History of the Territory*. New York: the Lewis Publishing Company, 1901.

Glasscock, C.B. *Then Came Oil: The Story of the Last Frontier*. Indianapolis: Bobbs-Merrill Company, 1938.

Haley, J. Evetts. *Fort Concho and the Texas Frontier*. San Angelo, Texas: *San Angelo Standard-Times*, 1952.

Harkey, Dee. *Mean as Hell*. Albuquerque: University of New Mexico Press, 1948.

Harman, S.W. *Hell on the Border: He Hanged Eighty-Eight Men*. Fort Smith, Arkansas: The Phoenix Publishing Company, 1898.

Harrington, Fred Harvey. *Hanging Judge*. Caldwell, Idaho: The Caxton Printers, Ltd., 1951.

Johnson, Nicholas. *Negroes and the Gun: The Black Tradition of Arms*. New York: Prometheus Books, 2014.

Katz, William Loren. *The Black West*. Garden City, New York: Doubleday and Company, Inc., 1971.

Leckie, William H. *The Buffalo Soldiers: A Narrative of the Negro Cavalry of the West*. Norman, Oklahoma: University of Oklahoma Press, 1967.

Schubert, Frank N. *Voices of the Buffalo Soldiers*. Albuquerque: University of New Mexico Press, 2003.

Owens, Ron. *Oklahoma Heroes: A Tribute to Fallen Law Enforcement Officers*. Turner Publishing, 2000.

Prassel, Frank Richard. *The Great American Outlaw: A Legacy of Fact and Fiction*. Norman, Oklahoma: University of Oklahoma Press, 1993.

Ricky, Don, Jr. *Forty Miles a Day on Beans and Hay: The Enlisted Soldier Fighting the Indian Wars*. Norman, Oklahoma: University of Oklahoma Press, 1963.

Shirley, Glenn. *Henry Starr: Last of the Real Badmen*. New York: David McKay Company, Inc., 1965.

Shirley, Glenn. *Law West of Fort Smith: A History of Frontier Justice in the Indian Territory, 1834-1896*. New York: Henry Holt and Company, 1957.

Shirley, Glenn. *Toughest of Them All*. Albuquerque: University of New Mexico Press, 1953.

Shirley, Glenn. *Marauders of the Indian Nations: The Bill Cook Gang and Cherokee Bill*. Stillwater, Oklahoma. Barbed Wire Press, 1994.

Sullivan, W.J.L. *Twelve Years in the Saddle for Law and Order on the Frontiers of Texas*. Austin: von Boeckman-Jones Company, Printers 1909.

Teal, Kaye M. *Black History in Oklahoma*. Oklahoma City: Oklahoma City Public Schools, 1971.

Wellman, Paul I. *Dynasty of Western Outlaws.* Garden City, New York. Doubleday and Company, Inc., 1961,

History of Nowata, Nowata County, Oklahoma, Historical Socieity.

Index

X

Y

Art T. Burton – Biography

Art T. Burton received a B.A. and a M.A. in African American Studies from Governors State University. He retired in 2015 after spending 38 years in higher education, as a history teacher, at Prairie State College and South Suburban College and administrator in African American Student Affairs at Benedictine University, Loyola University Chicago and Columbia College Chicago.

In 1991, Burton wrote the first book on African American and Native American outlaw and lawmen in the Wild West. It is titled *Black, Red and Deadly: Black and Indian Gunfighters of the Indian Territory, 1870-1907.* In 1999, Burton wrote the first book on African Americans who were scouts and soldiers in the Wild West. The book is titled *Black Buckskin and Blue: African American Scouts and Soldiers on the Western Frontier.* In 2007, Burton wrote the first scholarly biography on an African American lawman of the Wild West. This work is titled, *Black Gun, Silver Star: The Life and Legend of Frontier Marshal Bass Reeves.*

Some of the honors Mr. Burton has received include being named a "Territorial Marshal" by Gov. David Walters of Oklahoma in 1995; being inducted into "Who's Who in Black Chicago" in 2007; inducted into the Hall of Fame at the National Multicultural Western Heritage Museum in Fort Worth, Texas in 2008; inducted into "Who's Who in America" in 2010; and was given the "Living Legend Award" by the Bare Bones Film Festival in Muskogee, Oklahoma in 2015."

Burton has appeared in four documentaries for the History Channel on cable television. He was a participant on BET's Teen Summit with Mario Van Peebles for discussion on the movie *Posse.* In 2015, Burton appeared on FOX Cables' *Legends and Lies* Series, episode title, "The Real Lone Ranger" and was a participant in the AHC Cable series *Gunslingers* episode on Bass Reeves. Burton spoke at the B. B. King Symposium at Mississippi Valley State University in the fall of 2018 on African American and Native American cultures. In July 2019, Burton was the keynote speaker at the 10th Anniversary Bass Reeves Western History Conference in Muskogee, Oklahoma.

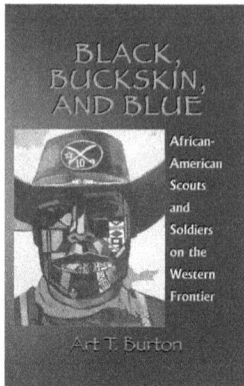